Standard Costing

ADVANCED MANAGEMENT AND ACCOUNTING SERIES
Series Editor: David Otley

Other titles in the series

Business Unit and Divisional Performance Measurement
MAHMOUD EZZAMEL

Capital Investment Decision-Making
DERYL NORTHCOTT

Accounting for Marketing
R. M. S. WILSON

The Social and Organisational Context of Management Accounting
A. G. PUXTY

Transfer Pricing
CLIVE EMMANUEL

Overhead Cost
FALCONER MITCHELL

Financial Planning Models
ROLAND KAYE

Information Systems for Management
DICK WHIDDETT

Principal and Agent Theory in Accounting
ANDREW STARK

Standard Costing

COLIN DRURY
The University of Huddersfield

|C| I |*m*|A|

Published in association with
The Chartered Institute of Management Accountants

ACADEMIC PRESS
Harcourt Brace Jovanovich, Publishers
London   San Diego   New York
Boston   Sydney   Tokyo   Toronto

This book is printed on acid-free paper

ACADEMIC PRESS LIMITED
24–28 Oval Road
LONDON NW1 7DX

United States Edition published by
ACADEMIC PRESS INC.
San Diego, CA92101

A catalogue
record for this
book is available
from the British
Library

ISBN
0–12–222355–1

Typeset by Photo·graphics
Printed in Great Britain by
Mackays of Chatham plc,
Chatham, Kent

Contents

Series Editor's Preface

David Otley
KPMG Peat Marwick Professor of Accounting
Lancaster University

A major problem for the management accounting teacher has been the selection of a suitable text for advanced courses. Although a number of very good texts exist, they typically do not include some topics that individual teachers wish to teach. On the other hand, they do include a considerable amount of material on topics that are unnecessary for a particular course. Students often feel that they have a poor deal in purchasing large and expensive texts that do not cover the whole of their course, yet include large amounts of extraneous material.

This series is an attempt to resolve this problem. It will consist of a set of slim volumes, each of which deals with a single topic in depth. A coherent course of study may therefore be built up by selecting just those topics which an individual course requires, so that the student has a tailor-made text for the precise course that is being taken. The texts are aimed primarily at final year undergraduate courses in accounting and finance, although many will be suitable for MBA and other postgraduate programmes. A typical final year advanced management accounting option course could be built around four or five texts, as each has been designed to incorporate material that would be taught over a period of a few weeks. Alternatively, the texts can be used to supplement a larger and more general textbook.

Each text is a free-standing treatment of a specific topic by an authoritative author. They can be used quite independently of each other, although it is assumed that an introductory or intermediate-level management accounting course has been previously taken. However, considerable care has been taken in the choice and specification of topics, to ensure that the texts mesh together without unnecessary overlap. It is therefore hoped that the series will provide a valuable resource for management accounting teachers, enabling them to design courses that meet precise needs whilst still being able to recommend required texts at an affordable price.

Preface

Since its introduction in the early 1900s standard costing has flourished and is now widely used by companies in the USA and Western Europe. It provides cost data which can be used for many different purposes such as inventory valuation, budgeting, cost control, decision-making and performance evaluation. This book aims to explain the nature and scope of standard costing and the principles involved in designing and operating a standard costing system.

The first chapter outlines the origins of standard costing, describes the operation of a standard costing system, its relationship to budgeting and control systems and explains the different purposes for which the data from a standard costing system can be used. Chapters 2 and 3 focus on the computation and interpretation of the full range of cost and sales variances which are presented in the current management accounting literature. Chapter 4 considers some of the criticisms which have been made against conventional variance analysis and discusses suggestions which have been made for providing a more meaningful approach to variance analysis. Chapter 5 explains the factors which should be taken into account in deciding whether or not it is worthwhile investigating variances and outlines some of the variance investigation models which have been presented in the accounting

literature. Chapter 6 focuses on how standard costs are recorded
in the accounts for stock valuation and profit measurement
purposes. In the final chapter the usefulness of traditional
standard costing techniques in today's competitive and advanced
manufacturing environment is assessed.

Throughout this book the illustrations have been kept simple.
More complex problems are presented in a section at the end of
the book which can be used by teachers to assess students'
understanding of specific standard costing topics. Answers to these
questions are available from the publishers to teachers who adopt
this book.

Finally, I would like to thank my wife Bronwen for converting
my original manuscript into a final typewritten form. My
appreciation also goes to the Chartered Association of Certified
Accountants, the Chartered Institute of Management Accountants
and the Institute of Chartered Accountants in England and Wales
for permission to reproduce the examination questions shown at
the end of this book.

1

The Nature and Scope of Standard Costing

Dictionaries define a **standard** as 'a definite level of excellence or adequacy required, aimed at, or possible.' In the accounting literature standards represent either target financial or physical inputs per unit of output. For example, a company which manufactures a range of kitchen furniture might establish the following standard inputs for the production of a particular kitchen table:

	£
Direct labour standard for one unit of output 4 labour hours at £10 per hour	40
Direct material standard for one unit of output 6 square metres of wood at £3 per square metre	18
Factory overhead standard 3 machine hours at £5 per hour	15
Standard cost of one unit of output	73

Standards are set based on predetermined physical inputs of labour, materials and machine hours which should be consumed in manufacturing a kitchen table. Predetermined target standard rates are applied to each input and standard labour, material and

1

overhead costs are established. The standard costs for each element of cost are added together to establish the product standard cost for one unit of output.

Standard costs thus represent predetermined costs; they are target costs which should be incurred under efficient operating conditions. They are not the same as **budget costs**. A budget relates to an entire activity or operation; a standard presents the same information on a per unit basis. A standard therefore provides expectations *per unit* of activity and a budget provides expectations for the *total activity*. If the budgeted output for a period is 1,000 tables the budgeted cost will be £73,000 and the standard cost will be £73 per unit.

ORIGINS OF STANDARD COSTING

Today's standard costing systems were developed in the early 1900s. It was the scientific management principles advocated by F.W. Taylor and other engineers who provided the impetus for the development of standard costing systems. Scientific management engineers developed information about standards in order to determine 'the one best way' to use labour and material resources. The standards provided information for planning the flow of work so that the waste of materials and labour was kept to a minimum. Scientific management engineers did not view standards as a tool to control financial costs.

At about the same time as the scientific managers were refining their techniques for determining standards, articles advocating the use of standards for cost control were published (see, for example, Longmuir 1902; Garry 1903; Whitmore 1908). According to Solomons (1968) it was G. Charter Harrison who, in 1911, designed and installed the first complete standard costing system known to exist.[1] In 1918 Harrison published the first set of equations for the analysis of cost variances. Much of Harrison's work is contained in today's literature on standard costing.

One more pioneer of standard costing is worthy of mention. In a series of articles in the Engineering Magazine of 1908 and 1909, Harrington Emerson advocated the development of an information system specifically directed towards the achievement of efficiency objectives. As part of his explanation Emerson noted the role that accounting was to play in this drive for efficiency. Emerson was possibly the first writer to stress that information about standards permits managers to differentiate variances that are due to controllable conditions and variances that are caused by conditions beyond management's control. This idea is contained in much of today's literature on responsibility accounting.

Since its introduction in the early 1900s standard costing has flourished and is now widely used by manufacturing companies throughout the USA and Western Europe. A survey of a wide cross-section of UK commercial and industrial organizations undertaken by Puxty and Lyall (1989) reported that 76% of the respondent companies operated a standard costing system. Why is standard costing used by most industrial companies? A major reason for its widespread use is that standard cost data can be used for many different purposes such as budgeting, control and inventory valuation. We shall discuss the various purposes for which standard costing systems can be used later in this chapter. At this point, however, it is appropriate to describe first the operation of a standard costing system.

OPERATION OF A STANDARD COSTING SYSTEM

Standard costing is most suited to an organization whose activities consist of a series of *common* or *repetitive* operations. It is therefore relevant in manufacturing organizations as the processes involved are often of a repetitive nature. Standard costing procedures can also be applied to non-manufacturing activities where operations are of a repetitive nature but it cannot be easily applied to activities of a non-repetitive nature, as there is no basis for observing repetitive operations and standards cannot be set.[2] A standard costing system can be applied to an organization which produces many different products, as long as production consists of a series of common operations. For example, if the output from a factory is the result of five common operations it is possible to produce many different product variations from these operations. It is, therefore, possible that a large product range may result from a small number of common operations. *Thus standard costs should be developed for repetitive operations* and product standard costs are derived by simply combining the standard costs from the operations which are necessary to make the product. This process is illustrated in Exhibit 1.1.

It is assumed that the standard costs are £50, £60, £70 and £80 for each of the operations 1 to 4. The standard cost for product 500 is therefore £200, which consists of £50 for operation 1, plus £70 and £80 for operations 3 and 4. The standard costs for each of the other products are calculated in a similar manner. In addition, the standard cost for the total output of each operation has been calculated. For example, six items of operation 1 have been completed giving a total standard cost of £300 for this operation (six items at £50 each). Three items of operation 2 have been completed giving a total standard cost of £180, and so on.

It can be seen from Exhibit 1.1 that different responsibility centres are responsible for each operation.[3] Hence, there is no point in comparing the actual cost of product 500 with the standard cost of £200 for the purposes of cost control, as three different responsibility centres (A, C and D) are responsible for the variance.

EXHIBIT 1.1

Standard costs analysed by operations and products

Responsibility centre	Operation No. and standard cost		Products							Total standard cost	Actual cost
			500	501	502	503	504	505	506		
	No.	Standard cost								£	
A	1	£50	√	√		√	√	√	√	300	
B	2	£60		√		√		√		180	
C	3	£70	√		√		√			210	
D	4	£80	√	√	√				√	320	
Standard product cost £			200	190	150	110	120	110	130	1,010	

None of the responsibility centres is *solely* answerable for the variance. Effective cost control requires that the standard and actual costs for a period are reported to the manager who is charged with the responsibility of the operation and the accompanying expenses. Therefore if the actual costs of responsibility centre A are compared with the standard cost of £300 for an output of six items, the manager of this responsibility centre will be accountable for the full amount of the variance. Note that the term variance is used to describe the difference between the standard and actual cost. *Only by comparing total actual costs with standard costs for each responsibility centre for a period can control be effectively achieved.* A comparison of standard *product* costs with actual *product* costs does not trace the variances to the specific individual who is charged with the responsibility for a particular operation. Variances analysed by products are thus inappropriate for effective accountability and cost control.

Figure 1.1 provides an overview of the operation of a standard costing system. You will see that the standard costs for the actual output for a particular period are traced to the managers of responsibility centres who are responsible for the various oper-

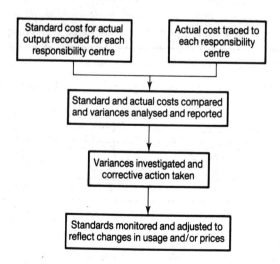

FIGURE 1.1 An overview of a standard costing system.

ations. The actual costs for the same period are also charged to the responsibility centres. Standard and actual costs are compared and the variance is reported. For example, if the actual cost for the output of the six items produced in responsibility centre A during the period is £450 and the standard cost is £300 (see Exhibit 1.1) a variance of £150 will be reported.

The operation of a standard costing system enables a detailed analysis of the variances to be reported. For example, variances for each responsibility centre can be identified by each element of cost (materials, labour and overhead) and analysed according to deviations from standard *usage* or the standard *prices* of these resources. The accountant assists managers by pinpointing where the variances have arisen and the responsible managers can undertake the appropriate investigations to identify the reasons for the variance. For example, the accountant might identify the reason for a direct materials variance as being due to excessive usage of a certain material in a particular operation, but the responsibility centre manager must investigate this process and identify the reasons for the excessive usage. Such an investigation should result in appropriate remedial action being taken or, if it is found that the variance is due to a permanent change in the standard, the standard should be changed.

It may be argued that there is little point in comparing actual performance with standard performance because such comparisons can only be made after the event. Nevertheless, if people know in advance that their performance is going to be judged against a standard, they are likely to act differently from the way they would have done if they were aware that their performance was not going to be measured. Furthermore, even though it is not possible for a manager to change his performance after the event, an analysis of how well a person has performed in the past may indicate, both to the person concerned and his superior, ways of obtaining better performance in the future.

ESTABLISHING COST STANDARDS

Control over costs is best effected through action at the point where the costs are incurred. Hence the standards should be set for the quantities of material, labour and services to be consumed in *performing an operation*, rather than the *complete product* cost standards. Variances from these standards should be reported to show causes and responsibilities for deviations from standard. Product cost standards are derived by listing and adding the standard costs of operations required to produce a particular product. For example, if you refer to Exhibit 1.1 you will see that the standard cost of product 500 is £200 and is derived from the sum of the standard costs of operations 1, 3 and 4.

There are two approaches which can be used to set standard costs. First, **past historical records** can be used to estimate labour and material usage. Second, standards can be set based on **engineering studies**. With engineering studies a detailed study of each operation is undertaken based on careful specifications of materials, labour and equipment and on controlled observation of operations. If historical records are used to set standards there is a danger that the standards will include past inefficiencies. Standards are set based on average past performance for the same or similar operations. Known excess usage of labour or materials should be eliminated or the standards may be tightened by an arbitrary percentage reduction in the quantity of resources required. The disadvantage of this method is that unlike the engineering method, it does not focus attention on finding the best combination of resources, production methods and product quality. Nevertheless standards derived from average historical usage do appear to be widely used in practice. Lauderman and Schaeberle (1983) conducted a survey of the cost accounting practices of large US companies and reported that 43% of the respondents used average historic usage to set material usage standards. In contrast, 67% used engineering studies, 11% used trial runs under controlled conditions and 15% used other methods.

Let us now consider how standards are established using the engineering studies approach.

Direct material standards

Direct material standards are based on product specifications which are derived from an intensive study of the input quantity which is necessary for each operation. This study should establish the most suitable materials for each product based on product design and quality policy, and also the optimal quantity which should be used after taking into account any wastage or loss that is considered inevitable in the production process. Material quantity standards are usually recorded on a **bill of materials**. A bill of materials describes and states the required quantity of materials for each operation to complete the product. A separate bill of materials is maintained for each product. The standard material product cost is then found by multiplying the standard quantities by the appropriate standard prices.

The standard prices are obtained from the purchasing department. The standard material prices are based on the assumption that the purchasing department has carried out a suitable search of alternative suppliers and has selected suppliers who can provide the required quantity of sound quality materials at the most competitive price. Normally price standards take into account the advantages to be obtained by determining the most economical order quantity and quantity discounts, best method of delivery and the most favourable credit terms. However, consideration should also be given to vendor reliability with respect to material quality and meeting scheduled delivery dates. Standard prices then provide a suitable base against which actual prices paid for materials can be evaluated.

Direct labour standards

To set labour standards, activities should be analysed by the different operations. Each operation is studied and an allowed time is computed, usually after carrying out a time and motion study. The normal procedure for a time and motion study is to analyse each operation to eliminate any unnecessary elements and to determine the most efficient production method. The most efficient methods of production, equipment and operating conditions are then standardized. This is followed by time measurements which are made to determine the number of standard hours which are required by an average worker to complete the job. Delays that are unavoidable such as machine breakdowns and routine maintenance are included in the standard time. Wage rate standards are normally either a matter of company policy or the result of negotiations between management and unions. The agreed wage rates are applied to the standard time allowed to determine the standard labour cost for each operation.

Overhead standards

Overhead costs cover a complex variety of many different costs, the individual components of which behave in different ways when activity increases or decreases. Some overhead costs such as power used to operate machinery vary directly and proportionately with activity. Other overhead costs such as the salaries of supervisors and the depreciation of factory buildings are largely independent of activity. Where overheads vary with activity it is appropriate to determine a **standard variable overhead rate** per unit of activity. With direct labour and materials the input requirement per unit of output is clearly defined and can be directly observed and studied in order to set targets. For example, with direct labour the standard usage might be two hours per unit of output. If the standard wage rate is £8 per hour then labour resources of £16 per unit output will be consumed. With variable overheads the cost of variable overhead resources per unit of output cannot be studied and measured. There is no observable direct relationship between resources required and units of output. It is, therefore, necessary to estimate the relationship using past data.

Variable overhead rates are estimated by examining past relationships between changes in departmental overhead costs and changes in departmental activity. However, several different activity measures exist. For example, variable overheads can vary with direct labour hours of input, machine hours, quantity of materials used, number of units of output and so on. The objective is to find the activity measure which exerts the greatest influence on cost.[4]

Various statistical tests can be applied to ascertain the relationship between different activity measures and variable overhead expenses. The activity measure which best explains cost variability should then be selected. For a detailed description of cost estimation techniques you should refer to Drury (1992, Chapter 22) or Scapens (1985, Chapter 4).

The activity bases for variable overheads which are most frequently used in practice are direct labour hours or machine hours. The variable overhead rate per unit of activity derived from the statistical analysis is applied to the standard labour or machine usage to derive a standard variable overhead cost per unit of output. Standard machine times per unit of output can be established using a similar approach to that described for determining standard labour times.

Fixed overheads are largely independent of changes in activity and remain constant over wide ranges of activity for a specified time period. It is, therefore, inappropriate for cost control purposes to unitize fixed overheads to derive a fixed overhead rate per unit of activity. However, in order to meet the external financial reporting stock valuation requirements, the Statement of Standard Accounting Practice on Stocks and Work in Progress (Accounting Standards Committee, SSAP 9) requires that fixed manufacturing overheads are traced to products. It is, therefore, necessary to unitize fixed overheads for stock valuation purposes. Standard fixed overhead rates are established for each production department by estimating the fixed departmental overheads for a period, usually a year. The budgeted fixed annual overhead is divided by the budgeted level of activity to derive a standard fixed overhead rate per unit of activity. The most frequently used activity bases are machine hours for machinery related overheads and direct labour hours for non-machine related overheads. The standard machine or direct labour hour rate is applied to the standard labour or machine usage per unit of output to derive the standard fixed overhead cost for a product. For example, if the budgeted fixed overheads and direct labour hours for a department are respectively £500,000 and 50,000 direct labour hours the standard fixed overhead rate would be £10 per direct labour hour. The standard fixed overhead cost for a product with a standard usage of two standard direct labour hours would be £20.

At this stage it is appropriate to summarize the approach which should be used to establish cost standards. *Control over costs* is best effected through action at the point where they are incurred. Hence standards should be set for labour, materials and variable overheads consumed in performing an operation. For stock valuation purposes it is necessary to establish *product cost* standards. Standard manufacturing product costs consist of the total of the standard costs of operations required to produce the product plus the product's standard fixed overhead cost. A standard cost card should be maintained for each product and operation. A typical product standard cost card is illustrated in Exhibit 1.2. In most organizations standard cost cards are now stored on a computer. Standards should be continuously reviewed and, where significant changes in production methods or input prices occur, they should be changed in order to ensure that standards reflect current targets.

EXHIBIT 1.2

An illustration of a standard cost card

Date standard set _____   Product: Sigma

Direct materials

Operation number	Item code	Quantity	Standard price £	Department A B C D	Totals £
1	5.001	5 kg	3	£15	
2	7.003	4 kg	4	£16	
					31

Direct labour

Operation number	Standard hours	Standard rate	Department A B C D	
1	7	£9	£63	
2	8	£9	£72	
				135

Factory overhead

Department	Standard hours	Standard rate		
B	7	£3	£21	
C	8	£4	£32	
				53
Total manufacturing cost per unit				£219

TYPES OF COST STANDARDS

The determination of standard costs raises the problem of how demanding the standards should be. Should they represent ideal or faultless performance or should they represent easily attainable performance? Standards are normally classified into three broad categories:

1. Basic cost standards.
2. Ideal standards.
3. Currently attainable standards.

Basic cost standards

Standards of this type represent constant standards which are left unchanged over long periods. The main advantage of basic standards is that a base is provided for a comparison with actual costs through a period of years with the same standard, so that efficiency trends can be monitored over time. When changes occur in methods of production, price levels or other relevant factors, basic standards are not very useful because they do not represent *current* target costs. For this reason basic cost standards are seldom used.

Ideal standards

These standards represent perfect performance. Ideal standard costs are the minimum costs which are possible under the most efficient operating conditions. Ideal standards are unlikely to be used in practice because they may have an adverse impact on employee motivation. Such standards constitute goals to be aimed for rather than performance that can currently be achieved.

Currently attainable standard costs

These standards represent those costs which should be incurred under efficient operating conditions. They are standards which are difficult, but not impossible to achieve. Attainable standards are easier to achieve than ideal standards because allowances are made for normal spoilage, machine breakdowns and lost time. The fact that these standards represent a target which can be achieved under efficient conditions, but which is also viewed as being neither too easy nor impossible to achieve, provides the best norm to which actual costs should be compared. Attainable standards can vary in terms of the level of difficulty. For example, if tight attainable standards are set over a given time period there might only be a 50% probability that the standard will be attained. On the other hand looser attainable standards might be set with a probability of 90% attainment.

Are demanding standards set in practice? In a survey of 100 large US companies Lauderman and Schaeberle (1983) reported that the majority of respondents described their labour and material standards as being 'attainable with average performance'. The following is a summary of their findings:

	Material standards %	Labour standards %
Level of performance attainable under the best possible combination of factors	10	7
Attainable with a high level of performance	29	29
Attainable with average performance	52	56
Attainable with below average performance	2.5	4
Other	6.5	4
	100	100

A similar survey, again in the USA, was undertaken by Cress and Pettijohn (1985). They reported that 50% of the companies surveyed used expected actual (but difficult to attain) standards, 42% used standards based on average past performance and 8% used maximum efficiency (ideal) standards.

PURPOSES OF STANDARD COSTING

Standard costing systems are widely used because they provide cost data for many different purposes. The following are the major purposes for which a standard costing system can be used:

1. To assist in **setting budgets and evaluating managerial performance**.
2. To act as a **control device** by highlighting those activities which do not conform to plan and thus alerting decision-makers to those situations that may be 'out of control' and in need of corrective action.
3. To provide a prediction of future costs which can be used for **decision-making** purposes.
4. To simplify the task of tracing costs to products for inventory valuation purposes.
5. To **provide a challenging target** which individuals are motivated to achieve.

Let us now consider each of the above purposese in more detail.

STANDARD COSTS AND BUDGETING

Standard costs are particularly valuable for budgeting because a reliable and convenient source of data is provided for converting the budgeted production schedule into physical and monetary requirements for materials, labour and other services. Budgets based on standard costs are likely to represent more reliable targets than when standard costs are not available. This is because standard costs are based upon careful studies of material usage requirements, operative methods, labour and machine times and variability of cost with volume. Standards have also been tested by comparing them with performance and ascertaining their reliability as appropriate targets. Hence they provide a good basis for predicting what performance can be expected in the future. Where an organization has not implemented a standard costing system a vast amount of work is necessary in order to determine responsibility centre budgets. Budgetary preparation time is considerably reduced if standard costs are available because the standard costs of operations and products can be readily built up into total costs for any budgeted volume and product mix. Managerial performance is often evaluated by measuring a manager's success in meeting budgets. In some companies bonuses are awarded which are based on an employee's ability to achieve the targets specified in the periodic budgets, promotion may be partly dependent upon a manager's budget record, or subordinates may consider it important to meet their budgets in order to gain approval from their superiors. We have seen that standards provide the source data for determining the budgeted performance. Setting standards and the reporting of variances, therefore, play an important role in evaluating managerial performance and thus can have a significant effect in influencing managerial behaviour.

STANDARD COSTING AND CONTROL

The major purpose of a standard costing system is to act as a control device by comparing actual and planned results and identifying significant deviations for remedial action. Devices of this kind are known as feedback control systems. The principles of feedback control systems can best be illustrated by a mechanical model such as a central heating system (see Figure 1.2) where differences between actual and desired warmth are used as signals for automatically changing boiler activity. You will see from Figure 1.2 that the feedback model consists of the following elements:

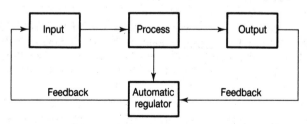

FIGURE 1.2 A mechanical control system.

1. The process (the room's temperature) is continually monitored by an automatic regulator (the thermostat).
2. Deviations from a predetermined level (the desired temperature) are identified by the automatic regulator.
3. Corrective actions are started if the output is not equal to the predetermined level. The automatic regulator causes the input to be adjusted by turning the heater on if the temperature falls below a predetermined level. The heater is turned off when the output (temperature) corresponds with the predetermined level.

The output of the process is monitored and whenever it varies from the predetermined level it is automatically adjusted. The elements of a mechanized feedback model can also be applied to a standard costing control system (see Figure 1.3). From this illustration you can see that the planned inputs for the actual output are compared with the actual results (that is, the actual inputs used) and deviations from the desired inputs are identified. The term **variance** is used to describe the difference between the desired and actual outcomes. Control reports are issued by the accountant to the managers responsible for controlling the inputs. Effective control requires that corrective action is taken so that actual results will conform with planned results in the future. Alternatively, the planned inputs may require modification if the comparisons indicate that the target (that is, the standards) can no longer be attained. Just as the thermostat compared actual and desired temperatures, the standard costing system must compare actual and planned performance to isolate deviation and enable corrective action to be taken.

The system of control described in Figure 1.3 is that of feedback control. **Feedback control** involves monitoring outcomes achieved against planned outcomes and taking whatever corrective action is necessary if a deviation exists. In **feed-forward control**, instead of actual outcomes being compared against desired outcomes, predictions are made of what outcomes are expected to be at some future time. If these expectations differ from what is desired control actions are taken which will minimize these differences. The objective is for control to be achieved before any deviations from desired outcomes actually occur. In other words

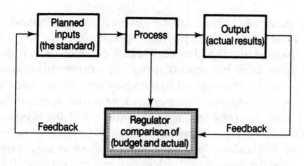

FIGURE 1.3 A standard costing control system.

with feed-forward controls likely errors can be anticipated and steps taken to avoid them whereas with feedback controls actual errors are identified after the event and corrective action is taken to implement future actions to achieve the desired outcomes.

The budgeting process is a feed-forward control system. To the extent that outcomes fall short of what is desired, alternatives are considered until a budget is produced that is expected to achieve what is desired. The comparison of actual results with planned results, identifying variances and taking remedial action to ensure future outcomes will conform with planned outcomes is an illustration of a feedback control system. Thus accounting control systems consist of both feedback and feed-forward controls.

STANDARD COSTS FOR DECISION-MAKING

For decision-making purposes, such as pricing or make or buy decisions, managers require estimates of future costs. Standard costs represent future target costs and thus provide a valuable source of information for decision-making purposes. Standard costs are preferable to estimates based on adjusted past costs since they are based upon the carefully determined usage of labour and materials. Product standards, therefore, should not include any avoidable inefficiencies. Standard costs are frequently used for pricing decisions. Many surveys of pricing procedures have reported that product costs play an important role in setting prices. This is particularly true for customized products which do not have readily available market prices. In competitive markets, selling prices are determined by competition and are outside the control of the supplier. However, a firm that can predict its product costs can concentrate on the most profitable product mix and avoid loss-making activities.

The use of standard costs saves clerical work in preparing cost information for pricing purposes and makes costs available to pricing executives more quickly than would be possible if standards were not available. Products priced on a bid basis may differ in some respects from products made before. However, there are usually parts, materials or operations which are the same as those used in products previously made. The existing standards are thus usually applicable for estimating costs of non-standard products.

We have noted that standard costs represent target costs that should be attained and thus do not include any avoidable inefficiencies. Hence they provide more appropriate information for pricing decisions because efficient competitors will seek to eliminate avoidable costs. It is, therefore, unwise to assume that inefficiencies are recoverable within the selling price.

STANDARD COSTING AND INVENTORY VALUATION

The Statement of Standard Accounting Practice on Stocks and Work in Progress (Accounting Standards Committee, SSAP 9) indicates that if standard product costs provide a reasonable approximation of actual product costs, they are acceptable for stock valuation calculations for external reporting.

Standard costs greatly simplify the task of tracing costs for inventory valuation purposes. Where a standard costing system has not been implemented it is necessary to maintain records at actual cost for each individual item of materials in store. In addition actual product cost records must be maintained in order to determine the valuation of finished goods and work in progress stocks. With a standard costing system it is unnecessary to maintain stores records and product costs at actual costs. Records are maintained at standard costs and the total standard cost can be obtained by multiplying the quantity of each type of material, component or product in stock by the appropriate standard unit cost. A considerable amount of data processing time is saved because stores records can be kept in terms of quantities only.

MOTIVATIONAL IMPACT OF STANDARDS

Standards represent targets which, under certain circumstances, individuals will be motivated to strive to achieve. The existence of defined quantitative targets is only likely to motivate higher levels of performance if they are accepted by the individuals responsible for achieving them. Then, and only then, will a standard motivate the desired behaviour. It is, therefore, important that we consider the factors that affect the motivational power of standards.

The level of difficulty of the standards

If we accept that the setting of targets can increase motivation we should consider at what level of difficulty the targets should be set. The research evidence indicates that when individuals are set very difficult targets they are unlikely to be accepted. They may perceive the target to be impossible to attain and give up, thus producing a performance which is worse than if a less demanding goal had been set. Alternatively, if very easy targets are set it is likely that the targets will be achieved but the individuals will not be motivated to achieve their full potential.

Hofstede's research (1968) provides a helpful insight into the effect targets set at different levels of difficulty have on aspiration levels (that is, an individual's own personal goal) and performance. He uses the diagram reproduced in Figure 1.4 to illustrate the effects. The diagram illustrates an expense budget (this budget is equivalent to the target or standard cost) where the level of expense is shown on the vertical axis and the degree of the tightness of the standard/budget is shown on the horizontal axis, going from very loose on the left to very tight on the right. The budget, aspiration levels and actual results are denoted by the letters, b, a and r. In the absence of a budget or target the expense level is assumed to be N, and the diagram shows what will happen if we consider various alternative budget levels from very loose (case 1) to very tight (case 6). In case 1 the budget is too loose (that is, above level N). The budgetee (that is, the person who is responsible for the budget) will not find the budget very challenging and will set a higher aspiration level (lower than the budgeted cost) but still above N. The result r will be equal to the aspiration level.

In case 2, the budget is equal to N, and the aspiration level and the result coincide with the budget; the budget will not influence performance. In case 3, the budget is below N and the budgetee responds by altering his or her aspiration level to below N but not to the budgeted level of expenditure. Because the aspiration level is not too difficult the actual result will be equal to the aspiration level. In case 4, the budget is tighter still and this results in an improvement in the aspiration level. However, since the budget and aspiration level are so tight, there is a strong possibility

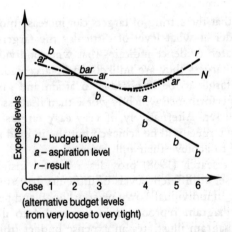

FIGURE 1.4 The effect of budget levels on aspiration levels.

that the actual result will not be as good as the aspiration level. Therefore *r* is shown to be above *a*, but the highest level of performance will be achieved at this point.

In case 5 the budget is very tight. The budgetee sees this as almost impossible and sets an aspiration level which is easier than case 4. In this situation the actual result will be equal to the aspiration level. In case 6 the budget is so tight that the budgetee will regard it as impossible. He or she will stop trying and will not attempt to set an aspiration level. The effect of this approach is that the actual result will be worse than that which would have been achieved had no budget been set.

A close examination of Figure 1.4 indicates that setting targets does not always lead to improved performance. In cases 1 and 6 the budgets do more harm than good, and improvements occur only in cases 3, 4 and 5. The problem is further complicated by the fact that failure to achieve the budget is likely to lead to a lowering of aspiration levels. Therefore, in case 4, where the actual result is worse than the aspiration level, the budgetee might respond by setting a less ambitious aspiration level next time.

Figure 1.4 implies that the target which motivates the best performance (case 4) is unlikely to be achieved much of the time. However, a target/budget which is usually achieved will motivate a lower level of performance (cases 1 and 2, in Figure 1.4). Therefore, if targets are to be set at a level which will motivate individuals to achieve maximum performance, adverse variances are to be expected. In such a situation it is essential that adverse variances are not used by management as a punitive device, as this is likely to encourage individuals to obtain easier targets by under performing or deliberately negotiating easily obtainable standards. This may lead to fewer adverse variances, but also to poorer overall performance.

To motivate the best level of actual performance demanding targets should be set and small adverse variances should be regarded as a healthy sign and not something to be avoided. If standard performance is always achieved with no adverse variances this indicates that standards are too loose to motivate the best possible results.

The research evidence suggests that cultural, organizational and personality factors all affect an individual's reaction to a budget target. Atkinson (1964) and McClelland (1961) observed that for persons with a high need for achievement (achievement motivation) the greatest intrinsic motivation (that is, satisfaction for a job well done) tends to result when effort is believed to have about a 50–50 chance of leading to good performance. In particular, feelings of accomplishment are associated with achievement of performance that is only in the 50% range of likelihood.

It would seem that easier targets do not represent a high enough challenge for persons with a high need for achievement. The fact that different individuals are likely to react differently to targets suggests that the optimum target level of difficulty should vary from individual to individual. However, in practice it may be impossible to personalize specific standards for different individuals.

Participation

It has been argued by many writers that by allowing employees to participate in setting targets it is more likely that the targets will be accepted than if they are imposed. For example, participation in the setting of standards may lead employees to feel a sense of ownership of the standards and to be more motivated to achieve the standards. However, the empirical studies have presented conflicting evidence on the usefulness of participation in the management process. There appears to be a number of important factors which influence how participation affects employees.

The research evidence suggests that participation in the standard setting process has been positively related to increased morale, better attitudes towards the budgeting system, the job and the organization (see Milani 1975; Collins 1978; Cherrington and Cherrington 1973). However, there is conflicting evidence on the relationship between participation and performance. Some studies (see Argyris 1953; Bass and Leavitt 1963; Kenis 1979) found that budgetary performance was better when budgetees participated in the budgeting process. On the other hand studies by Milani (1975) and Bryan and Locke (1967) found that participation appeared to lead to lower levels of performance.

These conflicting findings have prompted researchers to seek to determine the factors which influence the relationship between participation and performance. In a classic study Vroom (1960) demonstrated that personality variables can have an important influence on the effectiveness of participation. He found that participation was not effective for highly authoritarian people who prefer directive leadership and controlled unambiguous situations. In a more recent study Brownell (1981) argued that participation has a positive effect on performance particularly where people feel they have a large degree of control over their own destiny. The implications of these studies is that where organizations tend to have members with diverse characteristics, participation may be effective only if used discriminately and not applied across the board.

Feedback

Communication of variances between standard and actual performance provides information to employees to enable them to evaluate their performance against expectations and guides them to appropriate corrective action. Feedback on performance may enhance motivation partly through the greater degree of self-control that the feedback information provides, and partly through the feelings of achievement aroused by knowledge of what has been achieved. In general, feedback is positively associated with performance (see Cook 1968) but the relationship is complex and is dependent upon other factors. For example, the longer the delay in providing feedback information, the less the effect of feedback on performance. It is, therefore, important that feedback reports should be provided soon after a task has been completed so as to provide prompt feedback on any difference between standard and actual performance. Accounting control systems will lose their effectiveness if they fail to meet this requirement.

CONFLICTS IN KINDS OF STANDARDS USED

We have noted that to motivate higher levels of performance, challenging standards should be set with the possibility that the standard will not be attained. On the other hand, for budgeting, inventory valuation and pricing purposes less challenging standards should be set which are expected to be attained. For example, at the planning stage budgets are co-ordinated and the cash budget is prepared in order to ensure that sufficient cash is available at all times to meet the level of operations outlined in the various budgets. For budgetary planning purposes it is therefore important that planning is based on standards which are expected to be attained. Standard costs can be used for inventory valuation purposes only if they provide a reasonable approximation to actual costs. Standard product costs derived from tight challenging targets are also not helpful for pricing products as there is a high probability that the standard cost will not be attained. For inventory valuation and pricing purposes current standards based on attainable good performance standards should be used.

It is obviously impractical to have different sets of standard costs for each purpose. If challenging and tight standards are set for motivation purposes it is important to estimate the variances and incorporate these estimates in the budget and product cost standards in order to ensure that they reflect costs actually expected in the budget period. Thus, when standard costs do not provide exactly the costs needed for budgeting purposes, the forecast of variances provides a means whereby the standards can be utilized in preparing the budget without losing sight of the difference between standard costs and costs actually expected in the budget period.

If tight challenging targets are set in order to motivate maximum performance actual results should be compared with flexible budgets derived from these standards. On the other hand, the budgets set at the planning stage will have been derived from less challenging targets. There is a danger that budgetees may react unfavourably to a situation where they believe that one budget is used to evaluate their performance and a second looser budget is used for planning purposes. If top management consider that the conflict arising from using separate planning and motivation budgets outweighs the benefits arising from setting tight challenging motivation standards, it is appropriate to use one set of standard costs for all purposes. In this situation standards should be set based on attainable good performance.

FIXED AND FLEXIBLE BUDGETS

Cost control is exercised by reporting the difference between actual and planned costs, investigating the variance and taking appropriate corrective action so that actual results will conform with planned results in the future. Because some costs vary with changes in activity it is essential when reporting variances to take into account the variability of costs. For example, if the actual level of activity is greater than the budgeted level of activity then those costs that vary with activity will be greater than the budgeted costs purely because of changes in activity. Let us consider the simplified situation presented in Example 1.1.

EXAMPLE 1.1

The standard cost of an operation is as follows:

	£
Direct materials: 3 kg at £6 per kg	18
Direct labour: 2 hours at £8 per hour	16
Variable overheads: 2 direct labour hours at £3 per hour	6
	40

The budgeted output for the operation in department A for the period was 1,000 and the actual output was 1,200 units. Actual costs incurred were as follows:

	£
Direct materials: 3,600 kg at £5.50 per kg	19,800
Direct labour: 2,400 hours at £8 per hour	19,200
Variable overheads: 2,400 direct labour hours at £3 per hour	7,200
	46,200

You are required to compute the variances which should be reported for the period.

It is clearly incorrect to compare actual costs for the actual activity level of 1,200 units with budgeted costs for the budgeted activity level of 1,000 units. This incorrectly suggests the following overspending:

	Fixed budget based on 1,000 units	£	Actual (1,200 units output)	£	Variance £
Direct labour	1,000×2hr×£8 =	16,000	2,400hr×£8 =	19,200	3,200A
Direct materials	1,000×3kg×£6 =	18,000	3,600kg×£5.50 =	19,800	1,800A
Variable overheads	1,000×2hr×£3 =	6,000	2,400hr×£3 =	7,200	1,200A
		40,000		46,200	6,200A

The letter 'A' in the variance column signifies an adverse variance indicating that actual expenditure exceeds budgeted expenditure.

The above comparison incorrectly suggests an overspending of £3,200 for direct labour, £1,800 for direct materials and £1,200 for variable overheads. If managers are to be made responsible for the control of costs, it is essential that they are accountable under the conditions in which they worked, and not for a performance which is based on conditions when the budget was drawn up. In other words, *it is misleading to compare actual costs at one activity level with budgeted costs at another level of activity*. The original budget must be adjusted to the actual level of activity. This procedure is called **flexible budgeting**. The reported variances should be as follows:

	Flexed budget (based on output of 1,200 units)	£	Actual output (1,200 units)	£	Variance £
Direct labour	1,200×2hr×£8 =	19,200	2,400 hr×£8 =	19,200	nil
Direct materials	1,200×3kg×£6 =	21,600	3,600kg×£5.50 =	19,800	1,800F
Variable overheads	1,200×2hr×£3 =	7,200	2,400hr×£3 =	7,200	nil
		48,000		46,200	1,800F

The letter 'F' in the variance column signifies a favourable variance.

You can see that the budget has been adjusted to reflect what the costs should have been for an actual activity of 1,200 units. This indicates that £1,800 less expenditure has been incurred than would have been expected for the actual level of activity, and a favourable variance of £1,800 should be reported, not an adverse variance of £6,200, which would have been reported, if the original budget had not been adjusted. The term '**fixed budget**' is used to describe the situation where the original budget which was drawn up prior to the start of the budget period is compared with the actual results. In other words, a fixed budget is the budget for the *planned* level of activity and the budgeted costs are not adjusted to the *actual* level of activity. At this stage it is essential to note that for control purposes flexible budgets, and not fixed budgets, should be used to determine the standard costs of the operations for a period.

CONTROLLABLE AND NON-CONTROLLABLE COSTS

Costs are traced to each individual responsibility centre so that deviations from flexible budgets can be attributed to the person in charge. This system of cost accumulation is known as **responsibility accounting**. Responsibility accounting is based on the principle that it is appropriate to charge to an area of responsibility only those costs which are significantly influenced by the manager of that responsibility centre.

Frequently, the responsibility for a particular item of expense may be shared. For example, the *quantity* of raw materials used will be the responsibility of the manager of the production department, but the purchasing officer will be responsible for the *price* which is paid for these materials. We shall see that it is necessary to analyse variances by price and quantity so that they can be attributed to the appropriate managers. Conflict will arise if individuals who lack authority to control expenditure are incorrectly charged with the responsibility for its incurrence.

RELATIONSHIP BETWEEN BUDGETARY CONTROL AND STANDARD COSTING

The annual budgeting process ensures that managers plan for future operations, and they consider how conditions in the next year might change and what steps they should take now to respond to these changed conditions. The budget serves as a vehicle through which the actions of the different parts of the organization can be brought together and reconciled in a common plan. Budgets are prepared for each responsibility centre, aggregated up the organization hierarchy and combined to produce a budgeted profit and loss account, balance sheet and cash budget. The objective is to ensure that the combined parts produce an acceptable whole. Otherwise, further adjustments and budget recycling will be necessary until the budgeted profit and loss account, the balance sheet and cash budget prove to be acceptable.

The approved annual budget will be analysed by monthly or four-weekly control periods. Actual results are compared with flexed budgets for each period and variances are reported. How does a standard costing system fit into this process? We have noted that standard costs are derived after careful studies of resource requirements, and thus provide a reliable basis for predicting budgeted performance. Setting budgets, however, is not dependent upon standard costs being available. For example, the survey by Puxty and Lyall (1989) reported that 94% of the respondent companies operated a budgetary control system, while 76% of the companies used standard costing. However, if a budgetary control system is operated without a standard costing system the resulting budgets are likely to be far less reliable.

For performance evaluation and control purposes, actual costs should be compared with a flexed budget. Flexing the budget, at say monthly intervals, requires a sound knowledge of cost behaviour and accurate cost estimates per unit of output. Standard costs provide a useful source of data for producing reliable flexible budgets. If a standard costing system has not been implemented a vast amount of work is necessary in order to prepare flexible budgets. Furthermore the flexed budgets are likely to be less reliable than budgets derived from standard costs.

Operating a standard costing system enables variances to be analysed in far more detail than would be possible if standard costs were not available. For example, variances can be analysed by operations, different types of materials and labour grades, and price and quantity elements. If you refer to the flexible budget on page 26 you will see that the variance is £1,800F. For an output level of 1,200 units standard usage is 3,600 kilos, the same as the actual usage. However, the actual price paid per kilo was £0.50 less than the standard price thus accounting for the total variance of £1,800 (3,600 kg × £0.50). With a standard costing system we can pinpoint where the variance has arisen, identify the manager responsible (the purchasing manager in this illustration) and also pinpoint the areas which require investigation. In our example, the £1,800 favourable variance may be due to purchasing inferior quality materials or alternatively, the purchasing department may have negotiated a lower price with a new supplier. If the former applies, corrective action should be taken, whereas the latter situation requires a change in the standard in order to reflect the new source of supply. Standard costing is thus an aid to budgetary planning and control. The real benefit from implementing a standard costing system is that it leads to a refinement and improvement in the data which is available for budgetary planning and control.

SUMMARY

Since its introduction in the early 1900s standard costing has flourished and is now widely used in the USA and Western Europe. A major reason for its widespread use is because it provides cost data which can be used for several different purposes. In this chapter it has been shown that standard costing can be used to:

1. Assist in setting budgets and evaluating managerial performance.
2. Act as a control device.
3. Predict future costs which can be used for decision-making.
4. Simplify the task of inventory valuation.

5. Provide challenging targets which individuals are motivated
    to achieve.

Standard costing is most suited to organizations whose activities
consist of a series of common or repetitive operations. Control
over costs is best effected through action at the point where they
are incurred. Standards should, therefore, be set for the quantities
of materials, labour and services to be consumed in performing
each operation. Product cost standards are derived from the list
of operations required to produce each product.

   Standards can be set from an analysis of past performance of
similar operations or they can be derived from detailed engineering
studies of each operation. Different types of standard costs can be
established ranging from ideal standards to loose currently
attainable standards. Challenging tight standards are likely to be
preferable for motivating maximum performance but standards
with a higher probability of attainment are required for budgeting,
inventory valuation and decision-making purposes. If the same
type of standard is to be used for all purposes standards should
be set based on attainable good performance.

   For control purposes costs should be traced not to products,
but to responsibility centres and compared against flexed budgets.
Variances should be analysed by operations, type of expense and
price and quantity elements. Detailed analysis helps to pinpoint
the cause of the variances.

   A budgetary planning and control system is not dependent upon
a standard costing system being implemented. However, the
presence of standard costs enhances the data which is available for
budgetary planning and control purposes and enables variances to
be analysed in much more detail.

NOTES

1. This was for the Boss Manufacturing Company, Illinois, USA –
   makers of work gloves.
2. Examples of non-manufacturing standards include standard time
   required per 100 invoices typed in a typing pool, standard time per
   thousand letters sorted in a mail dispatch department and standard

time per 100 computer punched cards in a data processing department.
3. A responsibility centre relates to a unit of the organization which is headed by a manager who is held responsible for its performance.
4. The term 'cost driver' is frequently used to refer to the activity measure which exerts the greatest influence on cost.

2

Variance Analysis

In Chapter 1 we noted that a standard costing system provides data which can be used for several different purposes. This chapter focuses on how cost data produced by a standard costing system can be used as a control device. It concentrates on variance analysis. First, the variances which can be computed where stocks are valued on a variable costing basis are described. The latter part of this chapter compares a standard variable costing system with a standard absorption costing system. Throughout the chapter standard hours are used as a measure of output. The first requirement is, therefore, to understand the meaning of the term 'standard hours produced'.

STANDARD HOURS PRODUCED

Standard cost systems frequently express output in standard hours rather than in physical units of output. **Standard hours of output** (also called standard hours worked, standard hours allowed or output hours) represent the number of hours that should have been used to obtain any given quantity of output. For example, if a department produces 100 units of a particular product and the standard time allowed for each unit of output is 30 minutes, the output for the period can be expressed as 100 physical units of output or 50 standard hours (100 × ½ hour) of output.

Output is frequently expressed in standard hours because departments often produce more than one product. In such situations it is not appropriate to express output in physical units of production. Consider a situation where a department produces 100 units of product X, 200 units of product Y and 300 units of product Z. Clearly it is inappropriate to add the production of these items together because they are not homogeneous. Instead, standard hours can be used as a common denominator for adding together the production of unlike items.

Let us assume that the following *standard times* are established for the production of one unit of each of the following products:

Product X   5 hours
Product Y   2 hours
Product Z   3 hours

This means that it should take 5 hours to produce one unit of product X under efficient production conditions. Similar comments apply to products Y and Z. The production for the department will be calculated in standard hours as follows:

Product	Standard time per unit produced (hours)	Actual output (units)	Standard hours produced
X	5	100	500
Y	2	200	400
Z	3	300	900
			1,800

In the illustration we would expect the *output* of 1,800 standard hours to take 1,800 direct labour hours of *input* if the department works at the prescribed level of efficiency. The department will be inefficient if 1,800 standard hours of output are produced using, say, 2,000 direct labour hours of input.

VARIANCE ANALYSIS

It is possible to compute variances simply by committing to memory a series of variance formulae. If you adopt this approach, however, it will not help you to understand what a variance is intended to depict and what the relevant variables represent. In our discussion of each variance we will, therefore, concentrate on the fundamental meaning for the variance so that you can logically deduce the variance formulae as we go along.

All of the variances presented in this chapter are illustrated from the information contained in Example 2.1. Note that in this example we assume that the company produces a single product which requires one operation. We also assume that the company has only one production department. In practice companies produce many products, requiring different operations which are performed in more than one department. A truly realistic situation would, however, fill many pages and the same variance calculations would be illustrated for each department. A more realistic situation would not, therefore, provide any further insight into your understanding of variance analysis. In order to ensure that you can compute variances in multi–product situations we shall illustrate the variance computations using standard hours as a measure of output. Let us now consider the situation outlined in Example 2.1.

EXAMPLE 2.1

Sigma manufacturing company produces a single product which is known as beta. The product requires a single operation and the standard cost for this operation is presented in the following standard cost card:

Standard cost card for product beta

	£
Direct materials:	
4 kg of X at £2 per kg	8.00
2 kg of Y at £4 per kg	8.00
Direct labour (5 hours at £8 per hour)	40.00

		£
Variable overheads (5 hours at £2 per direct labour hour)		10.00
Total standard variable cost		66.00
Standard contribution margin		44.00
Standard selling price		110.00

Sigma Ltd plan to produce 12,000 units of beta in the month of May and the budgeted costs based on the information contained in the standard cost card are as follows:

Budget based on the above standard costs and an output of 12,000 units

	£	£	£
Sales (12,000 units of sigma at £110 per unit)			1,320,000
Direct materials:			
X 48,000 kg at £2 per kg	96,000		
Y 24,000 kg at £4 per kg	96,000	192,000	
Direct labour (60,000 hours at £8 per hour)		480,000	
Variable overheads (60,000 hours at £2 per direct labour hour)		120,000	792,000
Budgeted contribution			528,000
Fixed overheads			240,000
Budgeted profit			288,000

Annual budgeted fixed overheads are £2,880,000 and are assumed to be incurred evenly throughout the year. The company uses a variable costing system for internal profit measurement purposes.

The actual results for May	£	£
Sales (11,000 units at £112)		1,232,000
Direct materials:		
X 45,000 kg at £2.10 per kg	94,500	
Y 24,000 kg at £3.80 per kg	91,200	
Direct labour (58,000 hours at £8.20 per hour)	475,600	
Variable overheads	114,000	775,300
Contribution		456,700
Fixed overheads		238,000
Profit		218,700

Manufacturing overheads are charged to production on the basis of direct labour hours. Actual production and sales for the period were 11,000 units.

Exhibit 2.1 shows the breakdown of the profit variance (the difference between budgeted and actual profit) into the component cost and revenue variances which can be calculated for the standard variable costing system described in Example 2.1.

MATERIAL VARIANCES

The costs of the materials which are used in a manufactured product are determined by two basic factors: the price which was paid for the materials, and the quantity of materials which were used in production. This gives rise to the possibility that the actual cost will differ from the standard cost because the *actual quantity* of materials used will be different from the *standard quantity* and/or that the *actual price* paid will be different from the *standard price*. We can, therefore, calculate a material usage and a material price variance.

Material price variances

The starting point for calculating this variance is simply to compare the standard price per unit of materials with the actual price per unit. In Example 2.1 the standard price for material X was £2 per kg but the actual price paid was £2.10 per kg. The price variance is 10p per kg. This is of little consequence if the excess purchase price has been paid only for a small number of units of purchases. But the consequences are important if the excess purchase price has been paid for a large number of units as the effect of the variance will be greater.

The difference between the standard material price and the actual price per unit should therefore be multiplied by the quantity

Variance analysis for a variable costing system[1]

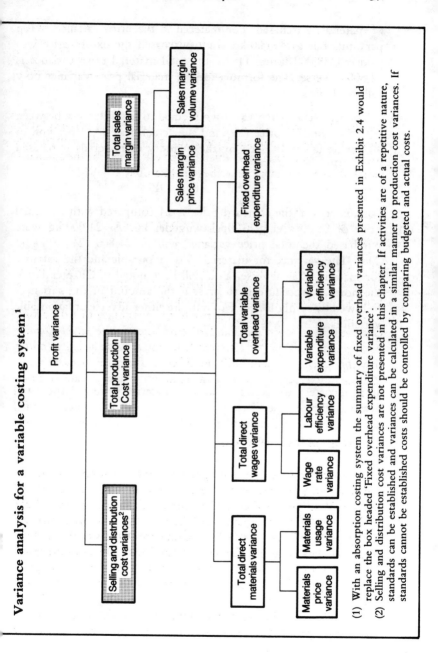

(1) With an absorption costing system the summary of fixed overhead variances presented in Exhibit 2.4 would replace the box headed 'Fixed overhead expenditure variance'.

(2) Selling and distribution cost variances are not presented in this chapter. If activities are of a repetitive nature, standards can be established and variances can be calculated in a similar manner to production cost variances. If standards cannot be established costs should be controlled by comparing budgeted and actual costs.

of materials purchased. For material X the price variance is 10p per unit, but as 45,000 kg were purchased the excess price was paid out 45,000 times. Hence the total material price variance is £4,500 adverse. The formula for the material price variance now follows logically:

The **material price variance** is equal to the difference between the standard price (SP) and the actual price (AP) per unit of materials multiplied by the quantity of materials purchased (QP), or:

$$(SP - AP) \times QP$$

For material Y the standard price is £4 compared with an actual price of £3.80 giving a 20p saving per kg. As 24,000 kg were purchased the total price variance will be £4,800 (24,000 kg at 20p). The variance for material Y is favourable and the variance for material X is adverse. You will have noted in Chapter 1 that the normal procedure is to present the amount of the variances followed by symbols A or F to indicate either adverse or favourable variances.

Possible causes

It is incorrect to assume that the material price variance will always indicate the efficiency of the purchasing department. Actual prices may exceed standard prices because of a change in market conditions which cause a general price increase for the type of materials used. The price variance might therefore be beyond the control of the purchasing department. Alternatively, an adverse price variance may reflect a failure by the purchasing department to seek the most advantageous sources of supply. A favourable price variance might be due to the purchase of inferior quality materials which may lead to a decline in product quality or more wastage. For example, the price variance for material Y is favourable but we shall see in the next section that this is offset by excess usage. If this excess usage is due to the purchase of inferior quality materials then the material usage variance should be charged to the purchasing department.

It is also possible that another department may be responsible for all, or part, of the price variance. For example, a shortage of materials resulting from bad stock control may necessitate an emergency purchase being made at short notice. The supplier may incur additional handling and freight charges on special rush orders and therefore may charge a higher price for the materials. In this situation the price variance will be the responsibility of the stores department and not the purchasing department.

Calculation on quantity purchased or quantity used

We have noted that price variances may be due to a variety of causes, some of which will be beyond a company's control, but others may be due to inefficiencies. It is, therefore, important that variances are reported as quickly as possible so that any inefficiencies can be identified and corrective action taken. A problem occurs, however, with material purchases in that the time of purchase and the time of usage may not be the same: materials may be purchased in one period and used in a subsequent period. For example, if 12,000 units of a material are purchased in period 1 at a price of £1 per unit over standard and 2,000 units are used in each of periods 1 to 6, the following alternative methods are available for calculating the price variance:

1. The full amount of the price variance of £12,000 is reported in *period 1* with quantity being defined as the *quantity purchased*.
2. The price variance is calculated with quantity being defined as the *quantity used*. The unit price variance of £1 is multiplied by the quantity used (that is, 2,000 units) which means that a price variance of £2,000 will be reported for each of *periods 1 to 6*.

Method 1 is recommended because the price variance can be reported in the period in which it is incurred, and reporting of the total variance is not delayed until months later when the materials are used. For the sake of simplicity we shall assume in Example 2.1 that the material purchases are identical to the material usage.

Material usage variance

The starting point for calculating this variance is simply to compare the standard quantity which should have been used with the actual quantity which has been used. In Example 2.1 the standard usage for the production of one unit of beta is 4 kg for material X. As 11,000 units of beta are produced, 44,000 kg of material X should have been used; however, 45,000 kg are actually used, which means there has been an excess usage of 1,000 kg.

The importance of this excess usage depends on the price of the materials. For example, if the price is 1p per kg, an excess usage of 1,000 kg will not be very significant, but if the price is £10 per unit, an excess usage of 1,000 kg will be very significant. It follows that to assess the importance of the excess usage the variance should be expressed in monetary terms.

Calculation based on standard price or actual price

Should the standard material price per kg or the actual material price per kg be used to calculate the variance? The answer is the standard price. If the *actual* material price is used the usage variance will be affected by the efficiency of the purchasing department as any excess purchase price will be assigned to the excess usage.

It is, therefore, necessary to remove the price effects from the usage variance calculation and this is achieved by valuing the variance at the standard price. Hence, the 1,000 kg excess usage of material X is multiplied by the standard price of £2 per kg, which gives an adverse usage variance of £2,000. The formula for the variance is as follows:

> The **material usage variance** is equal to the difference between the standard quantity (SQ) required for actual production and the actual quantity (AQ) used multiplied by the standard material price (SP), or:

$$(SQ - AQ) \times SP$$

For material Y the standard quantity is 22,000 kg but 24,000 kg have been used. The excess usage of 2,000 kg is multiplied by the standard price of £4 per kg which gives an adverse variance of £8,000. Note that the principles of flexible budgeting also apply here with *standard quantity being based on actual production and not budgeted production*. This ensures that a manager is evaluated under the conditions in which he actually worked and not those which were envisaged at the time the budget was prepared.

Possible causes

The material usage variance is normally controllable by the production foreman. Common causes of material usage variances include the careless handling of materials by production personnel, inexperienced or inefficient labour, the purchase of inferior quality materials, pilferage, changes in quality control requirements, or changes in methods of production. Separate material usage variances should be calculated for each type of material used and allocated to each responsibility centre.

Reporting

To ensure speedy reporting of variances, stores requisitions should be issued by the production planning department for the standard quantity of material which is required for each production order. This is obtained by referring to the output specified on the production order and multiplying by the material requirements per unit of output which are listed on the standard cost card. The stores department then issues the standard amount of material allowed. As production occurs, any additional materials which are required to complete the order may be issued only by submitting a supplementary excess materials usage requisition. This should be a different colour, with a distinctive code designation so that the variance is highlighted when the excess materials are issued. The stores requisition should contain a statement of the reasons for the excess usage and should be signed by the person who is responsible for the materials usage variance. If this procedure is followed the person responsible will quickly be made aware of any excess usage. If performance is better than expected, special material return requisitions should be used to signal favourable usage variances. A periodic summary of excess usage and material return requisitions should be prepared for departmental supervisors on a daily basis. These summary reports are often expressed in physical terms only.

Joint price usage variance

Note that the analysis of the material variance into the price and usage elements is not theoretically correct as there may be a joint mutual price/quantity effect. The following information is extracted from Example 2.1 for material X:

1. 44,000 kg of material X are required at a standard price of £2 per kg.
2. 45,000 kg are used at a price of £2.10 per kg.

The purchasing officer might readily accept responsibility for the price variance of 10p per kg for 44,000 kg but may claim that the extra 1,000 kg at 10p is more the responsibility of the production foreman. It may be argued that, if the foreman had produced in accordance with the standard, the extra 1,000 kg would not have been needed.

The foreman, on the other hand, will accept responsibility for the 1,000 kg excess usage at a standard price of £2 but will argue that he should not be held accountable for the additional purchase price of 10p per unit.

One possible way of dealing with this would be to report the joint price/quantity variance of £100 (1,000 kg at 10p) separately and not charge it to either manager. In other words the original price variance of £4,500 would be analysed as follows:

1. Pure price variance (44,000 kg at £0.10 per kg)	£4,400A
2. Joint price/quantity variance (1,000 kg at £0.10 per kg)	£100A
	£4,500A

The importance of this refinement depends on the significance of the joint variance and the purpose for which price variances are used. For example, if the purchasing officer is paid a bonus depending upon the value of the variance then conflict may arise where the purchasing officer's bonus is reduced because of the impact of an adverse joint price/quantity variance. Most textbooks recommend that the material price variance should be calculated by multiplying the difference between the standard and actual prices by the actual quantity, rather than the standard quantity. Adopting this approach results in the joint price/quantity variance being assigned to the material price variance. This approach can be justified on the grounds that the purchasing manager ought to be responsible for the efficient purchase of all material requirements irrespective of whether or not the materials are used efficiently by the production departments.

Total material variance

From Exhibit 2.1 you will see that this variance is the total variance before it is analysed into the price and usage elements. The formula for the variance is as follows:

> The **total material variance** is the difference between the standard material cost (SC) for the actual production and the actual cost (AC), or

$$SC - AC$$

For material X the standard cost is £8 per unit giving a total standard material cost of £88,000. The actual cost is £94,500 and, therefore, the variance is £6,500 adverse. The price variance of £4,500 plus the usage variance of £2,000 agrees with the total material variance. Similarly, the total material variance for material B is £3,200 consisting of a favourable price variance of £4,800 and an adverse usage variance of £8,000.

Note that if the price variance is calculated on the actual quantity *purchased* instead of the actual quantity *used*, the price variance plus the usage variance will agree with the total variance only when the quantity purchased is equal to the quantity which is used in the particular accounting period. Reconciling the price and usage variance with the total variance is merely a reconciliation exercise and you should not be concerned if reconciliation of the subvariances with the total variance is not possible.

LABOUR VARIANCES

The cost of labour is determined by the price which is paid for labour and the quantity of labour which is used. Thus a price and quantity variance will also arise for labour. Unlike materials, labour cannot be stored because the purchase and usage of labour normally takes place at the same time. Hence the actual quantity of hours *purchased* will be equal to the actual quantity of hours *used* for each period. For this reason the price variance plus the quantity variance should agree with the total labour variance.

Wage rate variance

This variance is calculated by comparing the standard price per hour with the actual price paid per hour. In Example 2.1 the standard wage rate per hour is £8 and the actual average wage rate is £8.20 per hour giving a wage rate variance of 20p per hour. To determine the importance of the variance it is necessary to ascertain how many times the excess payment of 20p per hour is paid. As 58,000 labour hours are used we multiply 58,000 hours by 20p. This gives an adverse wage rate variance of £11,600. The formula for the wage rate variance is as follows:

The **wage rate variance** is equal to the difference between the standard wage rate per hour (SR) and the actual wage rate (AR) multiplied by the actual number of hours worked (AH), or

$$(SR - AR) \times AH$$

Note the similarity between this variance and the material price variance. Both variances multiply the difference between the standard price and the actual price paid for a unit of a resource by the actual quantity of resources used.[1]

Possible causes

The wage rate variance may be due to a negotiated increase in wage rates not yet having been reflected in the standard wage rate. In a situation such as this the variance cannot be regarded as controllable. Labour rate variances may also occur because a standard is used which represents a single average rate for a given operation that is performed by workers who are paid at several different rates. In this situation part or all of the variance may be due to the assignment of skilled labour to work which is normally performed by unskilled labour. The variance may then be regarded as the responsibility of the foreman because he should have matched the appropriate grade of labour to the task at hand. However, the wage rate variance is probably the one that is least subject to control by management. In most cases the variance is due to wage rate standards not being kept in line with changes in actual wage rates and for this reason it is not normally controllable by departmental managers.

Labour efficiency variance

The labour efficiency variance represents the quantity variance for direct labour. The quantity of labour which should be used for the actual output is expressed in terms of *standard hours produced*. In Example 2.1 the standard time for the production of one unit of sigma is 5 hours. Thus a production level of 11,000 units results in an output of 55,000 standard hours. In other words, working at the prescribed level of efficiency, it should take 55,000 hours to produce 11,000 units. However, 58,000 direct labour hours are actually required to produce this output which means that 3,000 excess direct labour hours are used. We multiply the excess direct labour hours by the *standard* wage rate to calculate the variance. This gives an adverse variance of £24,000. The formula for calculating the labour efficiency variance is as follows:

The **labour efficiency variance** is equal to the difference between the standard labour hours for actual production (SH) and the actual labour hours worked (AH) during the period multiplied by the standard wage rate per hour (SR), or

$$(SH - AH) \times SR$$

This variance is similar to the material usage variance. Both variances multiply the difference between the standard quantity and actual quantity of resources consumed by the standard price per unit of resource consumed.

Possible causes

The labour efficiency variance is normally controllable by the production foreman and may be due to a variety of reasons. For example, the use of inferior quality materials, different grades of labour, failure to maintain machinery in proper condition, the introduction of new equipment or tools and changes in the production processes will all affect the efficiency of labour. An efficiency variance may not always be controllable by the production foreman; it may be due, for example, to poor production scheduling by the planning department, or to a change in quality control standards. The most suitable procedure for identifying the labour efficiency variance is for the job card to include the standard labour time for the particular operation. When the operation is completed the actual labour time is recorded and variances are coded and classified by cause so that the foreman is aware immediately of the variance. A periodic summary of the job cards should be prepared for the departmental supervisor on a daily basis. Daily summaries of efficiency variances are normally expressed in standard and actual labour hours and not in monetary terms.

Total labour variance

From Exhibit 2.1 you will see that this variance represents the total variance before analysis into the price and quantity elements.

The formula for the variance is as follows:

> The **total labour variance** is the difference between the standard labour cost (SC) for the actual production and the actual labour cost (AC), or

$$SC - AC$$

In Example 2.1 the actual production was 11,000 units, and with a standard labour cost of £40 per unit, the standard cost is £440,000. The actual cost is £475,600 which gives an adverse variance of £35,600. This consists of a wage rate variance of £11,600 and a labour efficiency variance of £24,000.

VARIABLE OVERHEAD VARIANCES

A total variable overhead variance is calculated in the same way as the total direct labour and material variances. In Example 2.1 the output is 11,000 units and the standard variable overhead cost is £10 *per unit* produced. The standard cost of production for variable overheads is thus £110,000. The actual variable overheads incurred are £114,000 giving an adverse variance of £4,000. The formula for the variance is as follows:

> **The total variable overhead variance** is the difference between the standard variable overheads charged to production (SC) and the actual variable overheads incurred (AC), or

$$SC - AC$$

It is normally assumed that variable overheads vary with direct labour or machine hours of *input*. The total variable overhead variance will, therefore, be due to one or both of the following:

1. A *price* variance arising from actual expenditure being different from budgeted expenditure.
2. A *quantity* variance arising from actual direct labour or machine hours of input being different from the hours of input which *should* have been used.

These reasons give rise to the two subvariances which are shown in Figure 2.1 – the variable overhead expenditure variance and the variable overhead efficiency variance.

Variable overhead expenditure variance

To compare the actual overhead expenditure with the budgeted expenditure it is necessary to flex the budget. Because it is assumed in Example 2.1 that variable overheads vary with direct labour hours of *input* the budget is flexed on this basis. (In Chapter 4 we shall consider a more refined approach which flexes the budget on the basis of *input* and *output*.) Actual variable overhead expenditure is £114,000 resulting from 58,000 direct labour hours of input. For this level of activity variable overheads of £116,000, which consist of 58,000 input hours at £2 per hour, should have been spent. Spending was £2,000 less than it should have been and the result is a favourable variance. If we compare the budgeted and the actual overhead costs for 58,000 direct labour hours of input we will ensure that any efficiency (quantity) content is removed from the variance. This means that *any difference must be due to actual variable overhead spending being different from the budgeted variable overhead spending*. The formula for the variance is as follows:

> The **variable overhead expenditure variance** is equal to the difference between the budgeted flexed variable overheads (BFVO) for the actual direct labour hours of input and the actual variable overhead costs incurred (AVO), or
>
> $$BFVO - AVO$$

Possible causes

The variable overhead expenditure variance on its own is not very meaningful. Any meaningful analysis of this variance requires a comparison of the actual expenditure for each individual item of variable overhead expenditure against the budget. The budgeted amounts are based upon expected prices and consumption rates for each variable cost item. It is possible for any combination of these items to change. For example, if indirect material costs are greater than budgeted costs, the difference may be due to an increase in the price of indirect materials, or to an increase in the rate of usage of these items, or a combination of both. Similarly, variable indirect labour costs may be different from the budget because of changes in wage rates or the rate of usage. These price and quantity differences may be traced to the same types of causes as those discussed earlier in this chapter in connection with direct labour and materials. Also, maintenance costs, power costs and other utilities may change because of rate changes or variations in consumption. Consequently, any meaningful interpretation of the expenditure variance must focus on individual cost items. If you refer to the performance report presented in Exhibit 2.6 (page 69) you can see how the £2,000 variable overhead expenditure variance should be analysed by individual items of expenditure.

Variable overhead efficiency variance

The variable overhead efficiency variance arises because 58,000 direct labour hours of input were required to produce 11,000 units. Working at the prescribed level of efficiency it should take 55,000 hours to produce 11,000 units of output. Therefore an extra 3,000 excess direct labour hours of input were required. Because variable overheads are assumed to vary with direct labour hours of input an additional £6,000 (3,000 hours at £2) variable overheads will be incurred. The formula for the variance is as follows:

The **variable overhead efficiency variance** is the difference between the standard hours of output (SH) and the actual hours of input (AH) for the period multiplied by the standard variable overhead rate (SR), or

$$(SR - AH) \times SR$$

You should note that if it is assumed that variable overheads vary with direct labour hours of input, this variance is identical to the labour efficiency variance. Consequently, the reasons for the variance are the same as those which have been described previously for the labour efficiency variance. If you refer again to Exhibit 2.1 you will see that the variable overhead expenditure variance (£2,000 favourable) plus the variable efficiency variance (£6,000 adverse) add up to the total variable overhead variance of £4,000 adverse.

Where it is assumed that variable overheads vary with machine hours the budget should be flexed on the basis of machine hours in order to calculate the variable overhead expenditure variance. The variable overhead efficiency variance is calculated as described above but machine hours are used instead of direct labour hours.

SIMILARITIES BETWEEN MATERIALS, LABOUR AND OVERHEAD VARIANCES

So far we have calculated price and quantity variances for direct material, direct labour and variable overheads. You will have noted the similarities between the computations of the three quantity and price variances. For example, we calculated the quantity variances (i.e., material usage, labour efficiency and variable overhead efficiency variances) by multiplying the difference between the standard quantity (SQ) of resources consumed for the actual production and the actual quantity (AQ) of resources consumed by the standard price (SP) per unit of the resource. In formula terms the quantity variances can be stated as:

$$(SQ - AQ) \times AP$$

The price variances (that is; material price, wage rate and variable overhead expenditure variances) were calculated by multiplying the difference between the standard price (SP) and the actual price (AP) per unit of a resource by the actual quantity (AQ) of resources acquired/used. In formula terms the price variances can be stated as:

$$(SP - AP) \times AQ$$

Alternatively this formula can be re-expressed as:

$$(AQ \times SP) - (AQ \times AP)$$

Note that the first term in this formula (with AQ representing actual hours) is equivalent to the budgeted flexed variable overheads which we used to calculate the variable overhead expenditure variance. The last term represents the actual cost of the resources consumed.

We can therefore calculate the price and quantity variances which have been illustrated so far in this chapter by applying the formulae outlined above. The formulae for the individual price and quantity variances described earlier in this chapter merely represent the same variance computations, with different symbols, in order to reflect the specific requirements of the individual variances and to enable you to concentrate on the fundamental meaning of each variance.

Fixed overhead expenditure or spending variance

With a variable costing system, fixed manufacturing overheads are not unitized and allocated to products. Instead, the total fixed overheads for the period are charged as an expense to the period in which they are incurred. Fixed overheads are assumed to remain unchanged in response to changes in the level of activity, but they may change in response to other factors. For example, price increases may cause expenditure on fixed overheads to increase. The fixed overhead expenditure variance, therefore, explains the difference between budgeted fixed overheads and the actual fixed overheads incurred. The formula for the variance is:

Budgeted fixed overheads less actual fixed overhead spending,
or

$$BFO - AFO$$

In Example 2.1 budgeted fixed overhead expenditure is £240,000 and actual fixed overhead spending is £238,000. Therefore the fixed overhead expenditure variance is £2,000. Whenever the actual fixed overheads are less than the budgeted fixed overheads the variance will be favourable. The total of the fixed overhead expenditure variance on its own is not particularly informative. Any meaningful analysis of this variance requires a comparison of the actual expenditure for each individual item of fixed overhead expenditure against the budget. The difference may be due to a variety of causes such as changes in salaries paid to supervisors, or the appointment of additional supervisors. Only by comparing individual items of expenditure and ascertaining the reasons for the variances can one determine whether the variance is controllable or uncontrollable. Generally, this variance is likely to be uncontrollable.

SALES VARIANCES

Sales variances can be used to analyse the performance of the sales function on broadly similar terms to those for manufacturing costs. The most significant feature of sales variance calculations is that they are calculated in terms of *profit or contribution margins* rather than *sales values*. Consider Example 2.2.

EXAMPLE 2.2

The budgeted sales for a company are 100 units at £11 per unit. The standard cost per unit is £7. Actual sales are 120 units at £10 per unit and the actual cost per unit is £7.

You will see that when the variances are calculated on the basis of sales *value* it is necessary to compare the budgeted sales *value* of £1,100 with the actual sales of £1,200. This gives a favourable variance of £100. This calculation, however, ignores the impact of the sales effort on profit. The budgeted profit contribution is £400 which consists of 100 units at £4 per unit, but the actual impact of the sales effort in terms of profit margins indicates a profit contribution of £360, which consists of 120 units at £3 per unit, indicating an adverse variance of £40. If we examine Example

2.2 we can see that the selling prices have been reduced, and that this has led to an increase in the total sales revenue but also to a reduction in total profits. The objective of the selling function is to influence favourably total profits. *Thus a more meaningful performance measure will be obtained by comparing the results of the sales function in terms of profit or contribution margins rather than sales revenues.*

Note that with a standard absorption costing system *profit* margins are used (selling price less total unit manufacturing cost) whereas with a standard variable costing system *contribution* margins (selling price less unit manufacturing variable cost) are used to calculate the variances.

Let us now calculate the sales variances from the information contained in Example 2.1.

Total sales margin variance

Where a variable costing approach is adopted the total sales *margin* variance seeks to identify the influence which the sales function has on the difference between budget and actual profit contribution. In Example 2.1 the budgeted profit contribution is £528,000 which consists of budgeted sales of 12,000 units at a contribution of £44 per unit. This is compared with the contribution from the actual sales volume of 11,000 units. Because the sales function is responsible for the sales volume and the unit selling price, but *not* the unit manufacturing costs, *the standard cost of sales and not the actual cost of sales is deducted* from the actual sales revenue. The calculation of actual profit for ascertaining the total sales margin variance will, therefore, be as follows:

Actual sales revenue (11,000 units at £112)	£1,232,000
Standard cost of sales for actual sales volume (11,000 units at £66)	£726,000
Actual profit contribution margin	£506,000

To calculate the total sales margin variance we compare the budgeted contribution of £528,000 with the actual contribution of £506,000. This gives an adverse variance of £22,000 because the actual contribution is less than the budgeted profit contribution.

The formula for calculating the variance is as follows:

The **total sales margin variance** is the difference between the
actual contribution (AC) and the budgeted contribution (BC)
(both based on standard unit costs), or

$$AC - BC$$

Using the standard cost to calculate both the budgeted and the
actual contribution ensures that the production variances do not
distort the calculation of the sales variances. The effect of using
standard costs throughout the contribution margin calculations
means that the sales variances arise because of changes in those
variables which are controlled by the sales function, that is, selling
prices and sales quantity. Consequently, Figure 2.1 indicates that
it is possible to analyse the total sales margin variance into two
subvariances – a sales margin price variance and a sales margin
volume variance.

Sales margin price variance

In Example 2.1 the actual selling price is £112 but the budgeted
selling price is £110. With a standard unit cost of £66, the change
in selling price had led to an increase in the contribution margin
from £44 per unit to £46 per unit. Because the actual sales volume
is 11,000 units, the increase in the selling price means that an
increased contribution margin is obtained 11,000 times, giving a
favourable sales margin price variance of £22,000. The formula
for calculating the variance is as follows:

The **sales margin price variance** is the difference between the
actual contribution margin (AM) and the standard margin
(SM) (both based on standard unit costs) multiplied by the
actual sales volume (AV), or

$$(AM - SM) \times AV$$

Sales margin volume variance

To ascertain the effect of changes in the sales volume on the difference between the budgeted and the actual contribution we must compare the budgeted sales volume with the actual sales volume. The budgeted sales are 12,000 units but the actual sales are 11,000 units, and to enable us to determine the impact of this reduction in sales volume on profit, we must multiply the 1,000 units by the standard contribution margin of £44. This gives an adverse variance of £44,000.

The use of the standard margin (standard selling price less standard cost) ensures that the standard selling price is used in the calculation, and the volume variance will not be affected by any *changes* in the actual selling prices. The formula for calculating the variance is as follows:

The **sales margin volume variance** is the difference between the actual sales volume (AV) and the budgeted volume (BV) multiplied by the standard contribution margin (SM), or

$$(AV - BV) \times SM$$

Difficulties in interpreting sales margin variances

The favourable sales margin price variance of £22,000 plus the adverse volume variance of £44,000 adds up to the total adverse sales margin variance of £22,000. It may be argued that it is not very meaningful to analyse the total sales margin variance into price and volume components because changes in selling prices are likely to affect sales volume. Consequently, a favourable price variance will tend to be associated with an adverse volume variance and vice versa. It may be unrealistic to sell more than the budgeted volume when selling prices have increased.

A further problem with sales variances is that the variances may arise from external factors and may not be controllable by management. For example, changes in selling prices may be the result of a response to changes in selling prices of competitors. Alternatively, a reduction in both selling prices and sales volume may be the result of an economic recession which was not foreseen when the budget was prepared. Manufacturing variances are not influenced as much by external factors and for this reason management are likely to focus most of their attention on the control of the manufacturing variances. Nevertheless, sales margin variances provide useful information which enables the budgeted profit to be reconciled with the actual profit. However, for control and performance appraisal purposes it is preferable to compare actual market share with target market share for each product. In addition the trend in market shares should be monitored and selling prices should be compared with competitors' prices.

Reconciliation of budgeted profit and actual profit

Top management will be interested in the reasons for the actual profit being different from the budgeted profit. By adding the favourable production and sales variances to the budgeted profit and deducting the adverse variances the reconciliation of budgeted and actual profit shown in Exhibit 2.2 can be presented in respect of Example 2.1.

Example 2.1 assumes that Sigma Ltd produces a single product consisting of a single operation and that the activities are performed by one responsibility centre. In practice, most companies make many products which require operations to be carried out in different responsibility centres. A reconciliation statement such as that presented in Exhibit 2.2 will, therefore, normally represent a summary of the variances for many responsibility centres. The reconciliation statement thus represents a broad picture to top management which explains the major reasons for any difference between the budgeted and the actual profit.

STANDARD ABSORPTION AND STANDARD VARIABLE COSTING

The UK Statement of Standard Accounting Practice (SSAP 9) requires that, for the purpose of external financial reporting,

EXHIBIT 2.2

Reconciliation of budgeted and actual profit for a standard variable costing system

	£	£	£	£
Budgeted net profit				288,000
Sales variances:				
Sales margin price		22,000F		
Sales margin volume		44,000A	22,000A	
Direct cost variances:				
Material–Price Material X	4,500A			
Material Y	4,800F	300F		
Usage Material X	2,000A			
Material Y	8,000A	10,000A	9,700A	
Labour–Rate		11,600A		
Efficiency		24,000A	35,600A	
Manufacturing overhead variances:				
Fixed overhead expenditure		2,000F		
Variable overhead expenditure		2,000F		
Variable overhead efficiency		6,000A	2,000A	
				69,300A
Actual profit				218,700

companies should value stocks at full absorption manufacturing cost. The effect of this is that fixed overheads should be allocated to products and included in the closing stock valuations. With the variable costing system fixed overheads are not allocated to products. Instead, the total fixed costs are charged as an expense to the period in which they are incurred.

Consider a situation where the fixed overheads for a period were £100,000 and the output was 10,000 units, of which 5,000 units were sold and the remaining 5,000 units are in stock. With a variable costing system fixed overheads of £100,000 will be charged as an expense to the period. With an absorption costing system fixed overheads will be unitized and allocated to products at £10 (£100,000/10,000 units) per unit of output. Therefore £50,000 (5,000 units at £10 per unit) fixed overheads will be charged as an expense to the period and the remaining £50,000 will be included in the closing stock valuation. Consequently the profit calculated on a variable costing basis will differ from the profits calculated on an absorption costing basis by £50,000. The profits reported will differ whenever the production and sales for a period are not identical. Identical profits will be reported whenever there are no stock movements and production equals sales. In order to neutralize the effect of stock movements it is assumed in Example 2.1 that production equals sales.

We have noted that published external accounts must be prepared on an absorption costing basis. However, where profits are measured at frequent intervals for internal reporting purposes there is a strong argument for adopting variable costing. For a discussion of the factors to be considered in selecting variable or absorption costing for internal profit measurement purposes refer to Drury (1992, Chapter 8).

So far we have considered the variances which arise from adopting a variable costing system. With an absorption costing system an additional fixed overhead variance is created. This variance is called a volume variance. In addition the sales margin variances must be expressed in unit profit margins instead of contribution margins.

STANDARD ABSORPTION COSTING OVERHEAD VARIANCES

With a standard absorption costing system predetermined fixed overhead rates are established by dividing annual budgeted fixed overheads by the budgeted annual level of activity.[2] We shall assume that in respect of Example 2.1, budgeted annual fixed overheads are £2,880,000 (£240,000 per month) and budgeted annual activity is 144,000 units. The fixed overhead rate per *unit* of output is calculated as follows:

$$\frac{\text{Budgeted fixed overheads (£2,880,000)}}{\text{Budgeted activity (144,000 units)}}$$

$$= \text{£20 per unit of beta produced}$$

We have noted earlier in this chapter that in most situations more than one product will be produced. Where there are different products, units of output should be converted to standard hours. In Example 2.1 the output of one unit of beta requires 5 direct labour hours. Therefore, the budgeted output in standard hours is 720,000 hours (144,000 × 5 hours). The fixed overhead rate per standard hour of output is:

$$\frac{\text{Budgeted fixed overheads (£2,880,000)}}{\text{Budgeted standard hours (720,000)}} = \text{£4 per standard hour}$$

By multiplying the number of hours required to produce one unit of beta by £4 per hour we also get a fixed overhead allocation of £20 for one unit of beta (5 hours × £4). For the remainder of this chapter output will be measured in terms of standard hours produced.

We shall assume that production is expected to occur evenly throughout the year. Monthly budgeted production *output* is, therefore, 12,000 units or 60,000 standard direct labour hours. At the planning stage an input of 60,000 direct labour hours (12,000 × 5 hours) will also be planned as the company will budget at the level of efficiency specified in the calculation of the product standard cost. Thus the **budgeted hours of input** and the **budgeted hours of output** (that is, the standard hours produced) will be the same at the planning stage. In contrast the *actual* hours of input may differ from the *actual* standard hours of output. In Example 2.1 the actual direct labour hours of input are 58,000 and 55,000 standard hours were actually produced.

With an absorption costing system fixed overheads of £220,000 (55,000 standard hours of output at a standard rate of £4 per hour) will have been charged to products for the month of May. Actual fixed overhead expenditure was £238,000. Therefore, £18,000 has not been allocated to products. In other words there has been an under recovery of fixed overheads. Where the fixed overheads charged to products exceeds the overhead incurred there will be an over recovery of fixed overheads. *The under or over recovery of fixed overheads represents the total fixed overhead variance for the period.* In formula terms the calculation of the total fixed overhead variance is identical to the calculation of the total direct labour and the total direct materials variance. The formula for the variance is as follows:

The **total fixed overhead variance** is the difference between the standard fixed overhead charged to production (SC) and the actual fixed overhead incurred (AC), or

$$SC\ (£220,000) - AC\ (£238,000) = £18,000A$$

Note that the standard cost for the actual production can be calculated by measuring production in standard hours of output (55,000 hours × £4 per hour) or units of output (11,000 units × £20 per unit).

The under or over recovery of fixed overheads (that is, the fixed overhead variance) arises because the fixed overhead rate is calculated by dividing *budgeted* fixed overheads by *budgeted* output. If actual output or fixed overhead expenditure differs from budget an under or over recovery of fixed overheads will arise. In other words the under or over recovery may be due to:

1. A fixed overhead expenditure variance arising from actual *expenditure* (£238,000) being different from budgeted *expenditure* (£240,000).
2. A fixed overhead volume variance arising from actual *production* differing from budgeted *production*.

The fixed overhead expenditure variance also occurs with a variable costing system. The favourable variance of £2,000 was explained earlier in this chapter. The volume variance arises only when stocks are valued on an absorption costing basis.

Volume variance

This variance seeks to identify that portion of the total fixed overhead variance which is due to *actual production* being different

from *budgeted production*. In Example 2.1 the standard fixed
overhead rate of £4 per hour is calculated on the basis of a normal
monthly activity of 60,000 standard hours per month. Only when
actual standard hours produced are 60,000 will the budgeted
monthly fixed overheads of £240,000 be exactly recovered. Actual
output, however, is only 55,000 standard hours. The fact that the
actual production is 5,000 standard hours less than the budgeted
output hours will lead to a failure to recover £20,000 fixed
overhead (5,000 hours at £4 fixed overhead rate per hour). The
formula for the variance is as follows:

The **volume variance** is the difference between actual
production (AP) and budgeted production (BP) for a period
multiplied by the standard fixed overhead rate (SR), or

$$(AP - BP) \times SR$$

The volume variance reflects the fact that fixed overheads do not
fluctuate in relation to output in the short term. Whenever actual
production is less than budgeted production, the fixed overhead
charged to production will be less than the budgeted cost and the
volume variance will be adverse. Conversely, if the actual
production is greater than the budgeted production the volume
variance will be favourable.

Sunk cost

Information which indicates that actual production is 5,000
standard hours less than budgeted production is useful to
management but to attach a fixed overhead rate to this figure is
of little value for control because fixed costs represent sunk costs.
The volume variance of £20,000 does not reflect the cost of the
facilities which remain idle as the fixed overhead cost will not
change if production declines, at least in the short term. A cost
of lost output only occurs if a firm has a demand for the lost
output. In this situation it is more meaningful to measure the cost
of the lost output in terms of the lost contribution from a failure
to produce the budgeted output (Horngren 1978). We shall
consider this approach in Chapter 4.

Possible causes

Changes in production volume from the amount budgeted may be caused by shifts in demand for products, labour disputes, material shortages, poor production scheduling, machine breakdowns, labour inefficiency and poor production quality. Some of these factors may be controllable by production or sales management while others may not.

When the adverse volume variance of £20,000 is netted with the favourable expenditure variance of £2,000 the result is equal to the total fixed overhead adverse variance of £18,000. *It is also possible to analyse the volume variance into two further subvariances – the volume efficiency variance and the capacity variance.*

Volume efficiency variance

If we wish to identify the reasons for the volume variance we may ask why the actual production was different from the budgeted production. One possible reason may be that the labour force worked at a different level of efficiency from that which was anticipated in the budget.

The actual number of direct labour hours of input was 58,000. Hence one would have expected 58,000 hours of output (that is, standard hours produced) from this input, but only 55,000 standard hours were actually produced. Thus one reason for the failure to meet the budgeted output was that output in standard hours was 3,000 hours less than it should have been. If the labour force had worked at the prescribed level of efficiency an additional 3,000 standard hours would have been produced and this would have led to a total of £12,000 (3,000 hours at £4 per standard hour) fixed overheads being absorbed. The inefficiency of labour is, therefore, one of the reasons why the actual production was less than the budgeted production. The formula for the variance is as follows:

> The **volume efficiency variance** is the difference between the standard hours of output (SH) and the actual hours of input (AH) for the period multiplied by the standard fixed overhead rate (SR), or

$$(SH - AH) \times SR$$

You may have noted that the physical content of this variance is a measure of labour efficiency and is identical to the labour efficiency variance. Consequently, the reasons for this variance will be identical to those previously described for the labour efficiency variance. Note also that as this variance is a subvariance of the volume variance the same comments apply as to the usefulness of attaching a value for fixed overheads, because fixed overheads represent sunk costs. Total fixed overhead will not change because of the efficiency of labour. Again it would be better to measure this variance in terms of the lost contribution arising from lost sales.

Volume capacity variance

This variance indicates the second reason why the actual production might be different from the budgeted production. The budget is based on the assumption that the direct labour hours of input will be 60,000 hours, but the actual hours of input are 58,000 hours. The difference of 2,000 hours reflects the fact that the company has failed to utilize the planned capacity. If we assume that the 2,000 hours would have been worked at the prescribed level of efficiency, an additional 2,000 standard hours could have been produced and an additional £8,000 fixed overhead could have been absorbed. Hence the capacity variance is £8,000 adverse.

Whereas the volume efficiency variance indicates a failure to utilize capacity *efficiently*, the volume capacity variance indicates a failure to utilize capacity *at all*. The formula is as follows:

The **volume capacity variance** is the difference between the actual hours of input (AH) and the budgeted hours of input (BH) for the period multiplied by the standard fixed overhead rate (SR), or

$$(AH - BH) \times SR$$

A failure to achieve the budgeted capacity may be for a variety of reasons. Machine breakdowns, materials shortages, poor production scheduling, labour disputes and a reduction in sales demand are all possible causes of an adverse volume capacity variance. Again, it is better to express this variance in terms of lost contribution from lost sales caused by a failure to utilize the capacity. It is not very meaningful to attach fixed costs to the variance as the total fixed costs will not be affected by a failure to utilize capacity.

Summary of fixed overhead variances

The volume efficiency variance is £12,000 adverse, and the volume capacity variance is also £8,000 adverse. When these two variances are added together they agree with the fixed overhead volume variance of £20,000. Exhibit 2.3 summarizes how the volume variance is analysed according to capacity and efficiency.

The actual *output* was 5,000 hours less than the budget giving an adverse volume variance. The capacity variance indicates that one reason for failing to meet the budgeted output was that 2,000 hours of *capacity* were not utilized. In addition, those 58,000 hours which were utilized only led to 55,000 hours of output. An *inefficient* use of the capacity, therefore, provides a second explanation as to why the budgeted output was not achieved. A fixed overhead rate of £4 per hour is applied to the physical quantity of the variances so that fixed overhead variances may be presented in monetary terms. Exhibit 2.4 summarizes the variances which we have calculated in this section.

In Example 2.1 we have assumed that fixed overheads are allocated to products on a direct labour hour basis. In automated production departments fixed overheads ought to be allocated on the basis of machine hours. Where machine hours are used as an allocation base output should be measured in standard machine hours and the fixed overhead variances calculated by replacing direct labour hours with machine hours.

We have noted that with an absorption costing system fixed overheads are allocated to products and this process creates a fixed overhead volume variance. *This variance is not particularly useful for cost control purposes* but we shall see in Chapter 6 that *the variance is required for profit measurement purposes.* Traditionally the volume

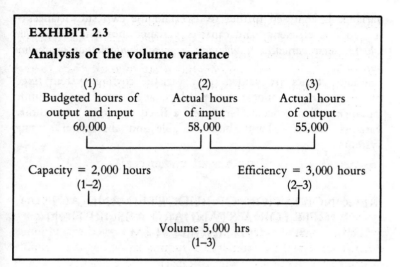

EXHIBIT 2.3

Analysis of the volume variance

| (1)
Budgeted hours of
output and input
60,000 | (2)
Actual hours
of input
58,000 | (3)
Actual hours
of output
55,000 |

Capacity = 2,000 hours   Efficiency = 3,000 hours
(1–2)   (2–3)

Volume 5,000 hrs
(1–3)

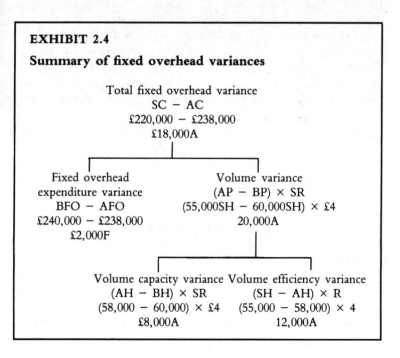

EXHIBIT 2.4

Summary of fixed overhead variances

Total fixed overhead variance
SC − AC
£220,000 − £238,000
£18,000A

Fixed overhead
expenditure variance
BFO − AFO
£240,000 − £238,000
£2,000F

Volume variance
(AP − BP) × SR
(55,000SH − 60,000SH) × £4
20,000A

Volume capacity variance
(AH − BH) × SR
(58,000 − 60,000) × £4
£8,000A

Volume efficiency variance
(SH − AH) × R
(55,000 − 58,000) × 4
12,000A

variance is analysed further to ascertain the two subvariances –
the volume efficiency and capacity variance, but it is *questionable
whether these variances provide any meaningful information for control
purposes.*

Where stocks are valued on a variable costing system fixed
overheads are not allocated to products and, therefore, a volume
variance will not occur. However, a fixed overhead expenditure
variance will arise with both variable and absorption costing
systems.

RECONCILIATION OF BUDGETED AND ACTUAL PROFIT FOR A STANDARD ABSORPTION COSTING SYSTEM

The reconciliation of the budgeted and actual profit is shown in
Exhibit 2.5. Note that the reconciliation statement is identical to
the variable costing reconciliation statement apart from the fact
that the absorption costing statement includes the fixed overhead
volume variance and values the sales margin volume variance at
the standard profit margin per unit instead of the contribution per
unit. If you refer back to page 35 you will see that the contribution
margin for beta is £44 per unit sold whereas the profit margin
per unit after deducting fixed overhead cost is £24. Multiplying
the difference in budgeted and actual sales volume of 1,000 units
by the standard profit margin gives a sales volume margin variance
of £24,000. Note that the sales margin price variance is identical
with both systems.

PERFORMANCE REPORTS

The managers of responsibility centres will require a more detailed
analysis of the variances to enable them to exercise effective
control, and detailed performance reports should be prepared at
monthly or weekly intervals to bring to their attention any

EXHIBIT 2.5

Reconciliation of budgeted and actual profit for a standard absorption costing system

	£	£	£	£
Budgeted net profit				288,000
Sales variances:				
Sales margin price		22,000F		
Sales margin volume		24,000A	2,000A	
Direct cost variances:				
Material–Price: Material X	4,500A			
Material Y	4,800F	300F		
Usage: Material X	2,000A			
Material Y	8,000A	10,000A	9,700A	
Labour–Rate		11,600A		
Efficiency		24,000A	35,600A	
Manufacturing overhead variances:				
Fixed–Expenditure	2,000F			
Volume capacity	8,000A			
Volume efficiency	12,000A	18,000A		
Variable–Expenditure	2,000F			
Efficiency	6,000A	4,000A	22,000A	69,300A
Actual profit				218,700

significant variances. A typical performance report based on the information contained in Example 2.1 is presented in Exhibit 2.6. A departmental performance report should include only those items which the responsibility manager can control or influence. The material price variances and the monetary amount of the volume variance are *not* presented as these are not considered to be within the control of the manager of the responsibility centre. However, the volume variance and the two subvariances (capacity and efficiency) are restated in non-monetary terms in Exhibit 2.6. You can see that these variances have been replaced by the following three control ratios:

Production volume ratio	$\dfrac{\text{Standard hours of actual output (55,000)}}{\text{Budgeted hours of output (60,000)}} \times$
	$100 = 91.7\%$
Efficiency ratio	$\dfrac{\text{Standard hours of actual output (55,000)}}{\text{Actual hours worked (58,000)}}$
	$\times\ 100 = 94.8\%$
Capacity usage ratio	$\dfrac{\text{Actual hours worked (58,000)}}{\text{Budgeted hours of input (60,000)}} \times 100$
	$= 96.7\%$

You can interpret these ratios in the same way as was described for the equivalent monetary variances. The ratios merely represent the replacement of an *absolute* monetary measure with a *relative* performance measure.

A comparison of current variances with those of previous periods and/or with those of the year to date is presented in the summary of the performance report. This information is often useful in establishing a framework within which current variances can be evaluated. In addition to monthly performance reports the manager of a responsibility centre ought to receive daily reports on those variances which are controllable on a daily basis. This normally applies to material usage and labour efficiency. For these variances the weekly or monthly performance reports will provide a summary of the information that has previously been reported on a daily basis.

SUMMARY

In this chapter we have explained the variance computations for a standard variable and a standard absorption costing system. With a standard variable costing system fixed overheads are not allocated to products. Sales margin variances are, therefore, reported in terms of contribution margins and a single fixed overhead variance; that is the fixed overhead expenditure variance is reported. With a standard absorption costing system fixed overheads are allocated

EXHIBIT 2.6
A typical performance report

DEPARTMENTAL PERFORMANCE REPORT

Department _____
Period _____ May 19 _____

Actual production   55,000   standard hours
Actual working hours   58,000   hours
Budgeted hours   60,000   hours

Control ratios: Efficiency 94.8%   Capacity 96.7%   Volume 91.7%

DIRECT MATERIALS

Type	Standard quantity	Actual quantity	Difference	Standard price	Usage variance	Reason
X	44,000	45,000	1,000	£2	£2000A	
Y	22,000	24,000	2,000	£4	£8000A	

DIRECT LABOUR

Grade	Standard hours	Actual hours	Difference	Standard cost	Actual cost	Total variance	Analysis Efficiency	Rate	Reason
	55,000	58,000	3,000	£440,000	£475,600	£35,600A	£24,000A	£11,600A	

OVERHEADS

	Allowed cost	Actual cost	Expenditure variance	Reason	Variable overhead efficiency variance	
					Hours	£
Controllable costs (variable):						
Indirect labour					Difference	
Power					between	3,000 6,000A
Maintenance					standard	
Indirect materials					hours and	
					actual	
					hours at	
					£2 per	
					hour	
Total	£116,000	£114,000	£2,000F		3,000	6,000A
Uncontrollable costs (fixed):						
Lighting and heating						
Depreciation						
Supervision						
	£240,000	£238,000	£2,000F			

SUMMARY	Variances (£)		Variances as a % of standard cost	
	This month	Cumulative	This month	Cumulative
	£	£	%	%
Direct materials	10,000A			
Direct labour:				
Efficiency	24,000A			
Wage rate	11,600A			
Controllable overheads:				
Expenditure	2,000F			
Variable overhead efficiency	6,000A			
Total	49,600A			

Comments:

to products and this process leads to the creation of a fixed overhead volume variance and the reporting of sales margin variances measured in terms of profit margins. The fixed overhead volume variance is not particularly helpful for cost control purposes but we shall see in Chapter 6 that this variance is required for financial accounting purposes.

To enable you to review your understanding of variance calculations the formulae for the variances which we have considered in this chapter are summarized below. In each case the formula is arranged so that a positive variance is favourable and a negative variance is unfavourable. The following variances are reported for both variable and absorption standard costing systems:

Materials and labour

1. Material price variance	(Standard price per unit of material − Actual price) × Quantity of materials purchased
2. Material usage variance	(Standard quantity of materials for actual production − Actual quantity used) × Standard price per unit
3. Total materials cost variance	(Actual production × Standard material cost per unit of production) − Actual materials cost
4. Wage rate variance	(Standard wage rate per hour − Actual wage rate) × Actual labour hours worked
5. Labour efficiency variance	(Standard quantity of labour hours for actual production − Actual labour hours) × Standard wage rate
6. Total labour cost variance	(Actual production × Standard labour cost per unit of production) − Actual labour cost

Fixed production overhead

7. Fixed overhead expenditure	Budgeted fixed overheads − Actual fixed overheads

Variable production overhead

8. Variable overhead expenditure variance	Budgeted variable overheads for actual input volume − Actual variable overhead cost
9. Variable overhead efficiency variance	(Standard quantity of input hours for actual production − Actual input hours) × Variable overhead rate
10. Total variable overhead variance	(Actual production × Standard variable overhead rate per unit) − Actual variable overhead cost

Sales margins

11. Sales margin price variance	(Actual unit contribution margin* − Standard unit contribution margin) × Actual sales volume
12. Sales margin volume variance	(Actual sales volume − Budgeted sales volume) × Standard contribution margin
13. Total sales margin variance	Total actual contribution − Total budgeted contribution

With a standard absorption costing system the following additional variances can be reported:

14. Fixed overhead volume variance	(Actual production − Budgeted production) × Standard fixed overhead rate

15.	Volume efficiency variance	(Standard quantity of input hours for actual production − Actual input hours) × Standard fixed overhead rate
16.	Volume capacity variance	(Actual hours of input − Budgeted hours of input) × Standard fixed overhead rate
17.	Total fixed overhead variance	(Actual production × Standard fixed overhead rate per unit) − Actual fixed overhead cost)

⋆ Contribution margins are used with a variable standard costing system whereas profit margins are used with an absorption costing system. With both systems actual margins are calculated by deducting *standard* costs from actual selling price.

NOTES

1. It is assumed that the quantity of material resources used is identical to the quantity of material resources purchased.
2. The activity measure selected should be the one which most closely determines the long-run overhead expenditure for a particular department. Most textbooks recommend direct labour hours for non-machine departments and machine hours for those departments where production is highly mechanized as a large proportion of overhead expenditure (e.g., depreciation) is likely to be related to machine utilization.

3

Mix and Yield Variances

In the previous chapter we focused on an illustration which assumed that a company employed a single grade of labour and operated a production process in which it was not possible to vary the mix of materials and deviate from engineered input–output relationships. We also assumed that our illustrative company produced and marketed a single product.

In this chapter we abandon these assumptions and extend our analysis to consider manufacturing processes in which it is possible to vary the mix of raw materials and direct labour skills. We also extend our analysis to consider situations where a company sells more than one product.

DIRECT MATERIALS MIX AND YIELD VARIANCES

In many industries, particularly of the process type, it is possible to vary the mix of input materials and affect the yield. Where two or more raw materials can be combined, input standards should be established to indicate the target mix of materials required to produce a unit, or a specified number of units, of output. Laboratory and engineering studies are necessary in order to determine the standard mix. The costs of the different material mixes are estimated and a standard mix is determined based on the mix of materials which minimizes the cost per unit of output but still meets the quality requirements. Trade-offs may occur. For example, cost increases arising from using better quality materials may be offset by a higher yield, or vice versa.

By deviating from the standard mix of input materials operating managers can affect the yield and cost per unit of output. Such deviations can occur as a result of a conscious response to changes in material prices or may arise from inefficiencies and a failure to adhere to the standard mix. By computing mix and yield variances, we can provide an indication of the cost of deviating from the standard mix.

Mix variance

The material mix variance arises when the mix of materials used differs from the predetermined mix which is included in the calculation of the standard cost of an operation. If the mixture is varied so that a larger than standard proportion of more expensive materials is used, there will be an unfavourable variance. When a larger proportion of cheaper materials is included in the mixture, there will be a favourable variance. Consider Example 3.1.

EXAMPLE 3.1

A company has established the following standard mix for producing 9 gallons of product A:

	£
5 gallons of material X at £7 per gallon	35
3 gallons of material Y at £5 per gallon	15
2 gallons of material Z at £2 per gallon	4
	54

A standard loss of 10% of input is expected to occur. Actual input was:

		£
53,000	gallons of material X at £7 per gallon	371,000
28,000	gallons of material Y at £5.30 per gallon	148,400
19,000	gallons of material Z at £2.20 per gallon	41,800
100,000		561,200

Actual output for the period was 92,700 gallons of product A.

The total input for the period is 100,000 gallons and using the standard mix, an input of 50,000 gallons of X (5/10 × 100,000), 30,000 gallons of Y (3/10 × 100,000) and 20,000 gallons of Z (2/10 × 100,000) should have been used. However, 53,000 gallons of X, 28,000 gallons of Y and 19,000 gallons of Z were used. Therefore 3,000 additional gallons of X at a standard price of £7 per gallon were substituted for 2,000 gallons of Y (at a standard price of £5 per gallon) and 1,000 gallons of Z (at a standard price of £2 per gallon). A material mix variance of £9,000 will, therefore, be reported. The formula for the material mix variance is as follows:

$$\text{(Actual quantity in standard mix proportions} - \text{Actual quantity used)} \times \text{Standard price}$$

If we apply this formula the calculation is as follows:

Actual usage in standard proportions:

	£
X = 50,000 gallons (5/10 × 100,000) at £7	350,000
Y = 30,000 gallons (3/10 × 100,000) at £5	150,000
Z = 20,000 gallons (2/10 × 100,000) at £2	40,000
	540,000

Actual usage in actual proportions:

	£
X = 53,000 gallons at £7	371,000
Y = 28,000 gallons at £5	140,000
Z = 19,000 gallons at £2	38,000
	549,000
Mix variance	£9,000A

Note that standard prices are used to calculate the mix variance to ensure that the price effects are removed from the calculation. An adverse mix variance will result from substituting more expensive higher quality materials for cheaper materials. Substituting more expensive materials may result in a boost in output and a favourable yield variance. On the other hand a favourable mix variance will result from substituting cheaper materials for more expensive materials but this may not always be in a company's best interests as the quality of the product may suffer or output might be reduced. Generally, the use of a less expensive mix of inputs will mean the production of fewer units of output than standard. This may be because of excessive evaporation of the input units, an increase in rejects due to imperfections in the lower quality inputs, or other similar factors. To analyse the effect of changes in the quantity of outputs from a given mix of inputs, a yield variance can be calculated. It is important that the standard mix is continuously reviewed and adjusted where necessary since price changes may lead to a revised standard mix. For an illustration of this approach see Wolk and Hillman (1972).

Direct materials yield variance

The **yield variance** arises because there is a difference between the standard output for a given level of inputs and the actual output which is attained. In Example 3.1 an input of 100,000 gallons should have given an output of 90,000 gallons of product A. (Every 10 gallons of input should produce 9 gallons of output.) In fact, 92,700 gallons were produced which means that the output was 2,700 gallons greater than standard. This output is valued at the average standard cost per unit of *output* which is calculated as follows:

Each 10 gallons of *input* is expected to yield 9 gallons of *output*. The standard cost for this output is £54.

Therefore standard cost for one gallon of *output* $= \dfrac{£54}{9} = £6$

The yield variance will be £6 × 2,700 = £16,200F. The formula is as follows:

$$\begin{array}{c} \text{(Actual yield − Standard yield from actual input of material)} \\ \times \text{ Standard cost per unit of output} = (92,700 \text{ gallons} \\ - \ 90,000 \text{ gallons}) \times £6 \end{array}$$

Adverse yield variances may arise from a failure to follow standard procedures. For example, in the steel industry a yield variance may indicate that the practice which was followed for pouring molten metal may have been different from that which was determined as being the most efficient when the standard yield was calculated. Alternatively, the use of inferior quality materials may result in an adverse yield variance.

The material mix variance in Example 3.1 is £9,000 adverse, while the material yield variance is £16,200 favourable. There was a trade-off in the material mix which boosted the yield. This trade-off may have arisen because the prices of materials Y and Z have increased whereas the actual price paid for material X is identical to the standard price. The manager of the production process may have responded to the different relative prices by substituting material X (the most expensive material) for materials Y and Z. This substitution process has resulted in an adverse mix variance and a favourable yield variance. Note, however, that actual material cost per unit of output is £6.05 (£561,200/92,700 gallons) whereas the standard cost per unit is £6 (£54/9 gallons). We shall see that this difference has been caused by an adverse material price variance.

At this stage you should be aware that materials price, mix and yield variances are interrelated and that individual variances should not be interpreted in isolation. Inter-dependencies should be recognized. You should also note that changes in relative input prices of materials will affect the optimal standard mix and yield of materials. Where significant changes in input prices occur the actual mix and yield should be compared with a revised ex post standard mix and yield. We shall discuss this approach in Chapter 4.

Material usage variance

The material usage variance consists of the mix variance and the yield variance. The material usage variance is, therefore, a favourable variance of £7,200 consisting of an adverse mix variance of £9,000 and a favourable yield variance of £16,200. To calculate the material usage variance we compare the standard quantity of materials for the actual production with the actual quantity of materials used and multiply by the standard material prices in the normal way. The calculations are as follows:

Standard quantity for actual production at standard prices:

Actual production of 92,700 gallons requires an
input of 103,000 gallons (92,700 × 10/9)
consisting of

		£
51,500 gallons of X (103,000 × 5/10) at £7 per gallon		360,500
30,900 gallons of Y (103,000 × 3/10) at £5 per gallon		154,500
20,600 gallons of Z (103,000 × 2/10) at £2 per gallon		41,200
		556,200 (i)

Actual quantity at standard prices:

	£
53,000 gallons of X at £7 per gallon	371,000
28,000 gallons of Y at £5 per gallon	140,000
19,000 gallons of Z at £2 per gallon	38,000
	549,000 (ii)

Material usage variance (i–ii)   £7,200F

Note that the standard quantity for actual production at standard prices can also be calculated by multiplying the actual output by the standard cost per unit of output (92,700 × £6 = £556,200).

Summary of material variances

The total material variance and the price variances are calculated using the approaches described in the previous chapter. The calculations are as follows:

Total material variance:

> Standard cost for actual production (92,700 × £6 = £556,200)
> − Actual cost (£561,200) = £5,000 adverse

Material price variances: (Standard price − Actual price) × Actual quantity

		£
Material X = (£7 − £7) × 53,000		nil
Material Y = (£5 − £5.30) × 28,000		8,400A
Material Z = (£2 − £2.20) × 19,000		3,800A
		12,200A

A summary of the variances is presented in Exhibit 3.1. We have already noted that these variances may be interrelated. The manager of the production process may have responded to the price increases by varying the mix of inputs which in turn may affect the yield of the process. The decomposition of the total material variance into price, mix and yield components highlights different aspects of the production process and provides additional insights to help managers to attain the optimum combination of materials input.

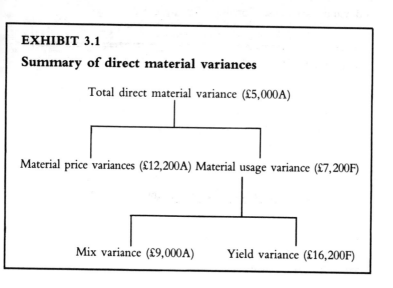

EXHIBIT 3.1

Summary of direct material variances

Total direct material variance (£5,000A)

Material price variances (£12,200A) Material usage variance (£7,200F)

Mix variance (£9,000A) Yield variance (£16,200F)

You should note that mix and yield variances are appropriate only to those production processes where managers have the discretion to vary the mix of materials and deviate from engineered input–output relationships. Where managers control each input on an individual basis and have no discretion regarding the substitution of materials it is inappropriate to calculate mix and yield variances. For example, there is often a predetermined mix of components needed for the assembly of washing machines, television sets and vacuum cleaners. In these production processes deviations from standard usage are related to efficiency of material usage rather than to changes in the physical mix of material inputs.

DIRECT LABOUR MIX AND YIELD VARIANCES

The same approach as that used to determine material mix and yield variances can also be applied to direct labour where it is possible to combine two or more grades of labour in order to perform specific operations. Where the manager of a production process has some discretion over the different grades of labour which can be used it is appropriate to calculate direct labour mix and yield variances. Consider Example 3.2.

EXAMPLE 3.2

Pursuing our previous example assume that the standard labour requirements for an output of 10 gallons of product A are:

2 hours skilled labour at £9 per hour	£18
3 hours unskilled labour at £7 per hour	£21
	£39

The actual output for the period was 92,700 gallons of product A and the actual direct labour hours of input were as follows:

20,000 hours skilled labour at £10 per hour	£200,000
26,000 hours unskilled labour at £6 per hour	£156,000
46,000 hours	£356,000

The standard labour cost per gallon of output is £3.90 (£39/10 gallons). We can now calculate the **total direct labour cost variance**. The calculation is:

Standard cost for actual output (92,700 × £3.90)	£361,530
Actual direct labour cost	£356,000
Total direct labour cost variance	£5,530F

The wage rate variance is calculated in the normal way:

Wage rate variance: (Standard rate − actual rate) × Actual hours

Skilled (£9 − £10)	× 20,000	£20,000A
Unskilled (£7 − £6)	× 26,000	£26,000F
		£6,000F

To calculate the **labour efficiency variance** we compare the standard quantity of labour hours for the actual production with the actual direct labour hours of input and multiply by the standard wage rate. The calculations are:

Standard labour hours for actual production at standard prices:

Actual production of 92,700 gallons requires an input of:

18,540 skilled labour hours (92,700/10 × 2 hrs) at £9 per hour	£166,860	
27,810 unskilled labour hours (92,700/10 × 3 hrs) at £7 per hour	£194,670	
	£361,530	(i)

Actual direct labour hours at standard prices:

20,000 hours of skilled labour at £9 per hour	£180,000	
26,000 hours of unskilled labour at £7 per hour	£182,000	
	£362,000	(ii)
Labour efficiency variance (i − ii)	£470A	

The labour efficiency variance can be subdivided into mix and yield variances in the same way as we subdivided the material usage variance in the previous section. The formula for **the mix variance** is:

(Actual input hours in standard proportions − Actual hours) × Standard wage rate

If we apply this formula the variance is calculated as follows:

Actual input hours in standard proportions:

Skilled labour = 18,400 hours (2/5 × 46,000 hours)
 at £9 per hour   £165,600
Unskilled labour = 27,600 hours (3/5 × 46,000 hours)
 at £7 per hour   £193,200
                                                                     £358,800

Actual input hours at standard wage rates:

Skilled labour = 20,000 hours at £9 per hour   £180,000
Unskilled labour = 26,000 hours at £7 per hour   £182,000
                                                                     £362,000

Mix variance   £3,200A

The adverse mix variance has arisen because more expensive, higher skilled labour has been substituted for lower skilled labour.

Let us now calculate **the yield variance**. An output of 10 gallons of product A is planned from each 5 hours of labour input. For an actual input of 46,000 hours an output of 92,000 gallons is expected (46,000/5 hrs × 10 gallons). The actual output for the period was 92,700 gallons thus resulting in an excess yield of 700 gallons. Multiplying the excess yield of 700 gallons by the standard labour cost per unit of output (£3.90) gives a favourable yield variance of £2,730. An alternative way of interpreting this variance is to work out the number of hours required to produce the actual output of 92,700 gallons. You will see that 46,350 hours (92,700/10 × 5 hours) are required. Thus 350 fewer hours were used and applying the average standard wage rate of £7.80 per hour (£39/5 hours) a saving of £2,730 would be obtained. In other words the yield variance shows that if the standard combination of skilled and unskilled labour hours were held constant the savings in labour costs would be £2,730.

Summary of labour variances

The total direct labour variance is £5,530 favourable and consists of a favourable rate variance of £6,000 and an adverse efficiency variance of £470. The £470 adverse efficiency variance consists of a £2,730 favourable labour yield variance of an adverse mix variance of £3,200. The favourable price variance has arisen from a decline in the wage rate of unskilled labour from £7 to £6 per hour and this has been only partially offset by an increase in the skilled wage rate. The favourable rate variance is negated somewhat by an adverse mix variance of £3,200 arising from substituting skilled labour for unskilled labour. A favourable yield variance though, of £2,730, arising from the total labour hours of input being less than the standard required to produce the actual output helped to reduce the overall efficiency variance to £470. A possible explanation is that many of the unskilled workers were new, earning lower than standard wage rate, and it was anticipated that they would be less efficient than the usual skilled workers. By using a mix with a higher proportion of skilled workers, the overall budget efficiency was almost attained. Again it is important to recognise the inter-dependencies between the variances.

SALES MIX AND SALES QUANTITY VARIANCES

Where a company sells several different products which have different profit margins, the sales volume margin variance can be divided into a sales quantity (sometimes called a sales yield variance) and sales mix variance. This division is commonly advocated in textbooks. The quantity variance measures the effect of changes in physical volume on total profits, and the mix variance measures the impact arising from the actual sales mix being different from the budgeted sales mix. The variances can be measured either in terms of contribution margins or profit margins.[1] However, contribution margins are recommended because changes in sales volume affect profits by the contribution per unit sold and not the profit per unit sold. Let us now calculate the sales margin mix and quantity variances. Consider Example 3.3.

EXAMPLE 3.3

The budgeted sales for a company for a period were as follows:

	Units	Unit contribution margin £	Total contribution £
Product X	8,000 (40%)	20	160,000
Y	7,000 (35%)	12	84,000
Z	5,000 (25%)	9	45,000
	20,000		289,000

and the actual sales were:

	Units	Unit contribution margin £	Total contribution £
Product X	6,000	20	120,000
Y	7,000	12	84,000
Z	9,000	9	81,000
	22,000		285,000

You are required to calculate the sales margin variances.

The **total sales margin variance** is £4,000 adverse and is calculated by comparing the difference between the budgeted total contribution and the actual contribution. Contribution margins for the three products were exactly as budgeted. The total sales margin for the period, therefore, consists of a zero **sales margin price variance** and an adverse **sales margin volume variance** of £4,000. Even though more units were sold than anticipated (22,000 rather than the budgeted 20,000), and budgeted and actual contribution margins were the same, the sales volume variance is £4,000 adverse. The reasons for this arises from having sold fewer units of product X, the high margin product, and more units of product Z which has the lowest margin.

We can explain how the sales volume margin variance was affected by the change in sales mix by calculating the **sales margin mix variance**. The formula for calculating this variance is:

$$(\text{Actual sales quantity} - \text{Actual sales quantity in budgeted proportions}) \times \text{Standard margin}$$

If we apply this formula we will obtain the following calculations:

	Actual sales quantity	Actual sales in budgeted proportions	Difference	Standard margin £	Sales margin mix variance £
Product X	6,000 (27%)	8,800 (40%)	− 2,800	20	56,000A
Y	7,000 (32%)	7,700 (35%)	− 700	12	8,400A
Z	9,000 (41%)	5,500 (25%)	+ 3,500	9	31,500F
	22,000	22,000			32,900A

To compute the sales quantity component of the sales volume variance we compare the budgeted and actual sales volume (holding the product mix constant). The formula for calculating the **sales quantity variance** is as follows:

$$(\text{Actual sales quantity in budgeted proportion} - \text{Budgeted sales quantity}) \times \text{Standard margin}$$

Applying this formula gives the following calculations:

	Actual sales in budgeted proportions	Budgeted sales quantity	Difference	Standard margin £	Sales margin quantity variance £
Product X	8,800	8,000	+ 800	20	16,000F
Y	7,700	7,000	+ 700	12	8,400F
Z	5,500	5,000	+ 500	9	4,500F
	22,000	20,000			28,900F

The sales quantity variance is sometimes further divided into a market size and a market share variance. A summary of the sales margin variances is presented in Exhibit 3.2. Before considering

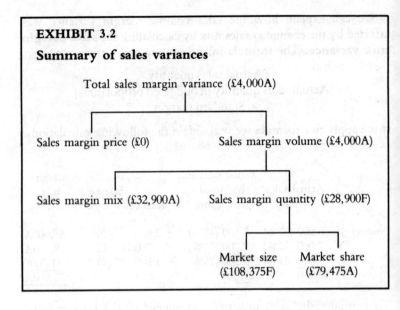

EXHIBIT 3.2

Summary of sales variances

the market size and market share variances we shall discuss the sales variances we have calculated so far in respect of Example 3.3.

By separating the sales volume variance into a quantity and mix variance we can explain how the sales volume variance is affected by a shift in the total physical volume of sales and a shift in the relative mix of products. The sales volume quantity variance indicates that if the original planned sales mix of 40% of X, 35% of Y and 25% of Z had been maintained, then for the actual sales volume of 22,000 units, profits would have increased by £28,900. In other words the sales volume variance would have been £28,900 favourable instead of £4,000 adverse. However, because the actual sales mix was not in accordance with the budgeted sales mix an adverse mix variance of £32,900 occurred. The adverse sales mix variance has arisen because of an increase in the percentage of units sold of product Z, which has the lowest contribution margin, and a decrease in the percentage sold of units of product X, which has the highest contribution margin. An adverse mix variance will occur whenever there is an increase in the percentage sold of units with below average contribution margins or a decrease in the percentage sold of units with above average contribution margins. The division of the sales volume variance into quantity and mix components demonstrates that increasing or maximizing sales volume may not be as desirable as promoting the sales of the most desirable mix of products.

Market size and share variances

Where published industry sales statistics are readily available it is possible to divide the sales quantity variance into a component due to changes in market size and a component due to changes in market share. Suppose that the budgeted industry sales volume for the illustrative company in Example 3.3 was 200,000 units and a market share of 10 per cent was predicted. Assume also that the actual industry sales volume was 275,000 units and the company obtained a market share of 8 per cent (8% × 275,000 = 22,000 units). The formulae and calculations of the market size and market share variances are as follows:

$$\begin{matrix} \text{Market} \\ \text{size} \\ \text{variance} \end{matrix} = \begin{bmatrix} \text{Budgeted} \\ \text{market} \\ \text{share} \\ \text{percent-} \\ \text{age} \end{bmatrix} \times \begin{bmatrix} \text{Actual} & \text{Budget} \\ \text{industry} & \text{industry} \\ \text{sales} & -\text{sales} \\ \text{volume} & \text{volume} \\ \text{in units} & \text{in units} \end{bmatrix} \times \begin{bmatrix} \text{Budgeted} \\ \text{average} \\ \text{contribution} \\ \text{margin} \\ \text{per unit} \end{bmatrix}$$

$$= 10\% \times (275{,}000 - 200{,}000) \times £14.45^*$$

$$= £108{,}375\text{F}$$

*Budgeted company total contribution (£289,000)/Budgeted sales volume in units (20,000)

$$\begin{matrix} \text{Market} \\ \text{share} \\ \text{variance} \end{matrix} = \begin{bmatrix} \text{Actual} & \text{Budgeted} \\ \text{market} & \text{market} \\ \text{share} & -\text{share} \\ \text{percent-} & \text{percent-} \\ \text{age} & \text{age} \end{bmatrix} \times \begin{bmatrix} \text{Actual} & \text{Budgeted} \\ \text{industry} & \text{average} \\ \text{sales} & \times \text{contribution} \\ \text{volume} & \text{margin} \\ \text{in units} & \text{per unit} \end{bmatrix}$$

$$= (8\% - 10\%) \times 275{,}000 \times £14.45$$

$$= £79{,}475\text{A}$$

The market size variance indicates that an additional contribution of £108,375 was expected, given that the market expanded from 200,000 to 275,000 units. However, the company did not attain the predicted market share of 10%. Instead, a market share of only 8% was attained and the 2% decline in market share resulted in a failure to obtain a contribution of £79,475. Hence the sum of the market size variance (£108,375F) and the market share variance (£75,475A) equals the sales margin quantity variance of £28,900.

Using the budgeted average contribution per unit in the formulae for the market size and share variances implies that we are assuming that budgeted and actual industry sales mix is the same as company's sales mix of 40% of X, 35% of Y and 25% of Z. Market size and share variances provide more meaningful information where the market size for each individual product can be ascertained.

Criticisms of sales margin variances

Sales margin price and volume variances and the decomposition of the volume variance into mix and yield variances are commonly advocated in textbooks. However, some writers (see, for example, Manes 1983) question the usefulness of sales variance analysis on the grounds that in an imperfectly competitive market structure, prices and quantities are interrelated. Given price elasticity, the logical consequence of lower/higher sales prices is higher/lower volume. Thus the relevant variances and analysis based on these variances are also interrelated. Consequently it is argued that sales margin variance analysis does not generate any meaningful results.

Several writers have also argued that it is inappropriate to separate the sales volume variance into mix and quantity variances. Bastable and Bao (1988) illustrate two different approaches which are advocated in the literature to calculate mix and yield variances. The first approach calculates weights in terms of physical quantities whereas the second uses sales dollars. Bastable and Bao show that the two approaches generate divergent results in many situations. Because of this deficiency they argue that decomposing the sales volume variance into mix and quantity variances is misleading and has the potential for doing more harm than good.

Peles (1986) has drawn attention to the problem of relying on an arbitrarily defined unit of product when the physical units method is used to calculate the sales mix and quantity variances. Where a firm sells a number of heterogeneous products the numerical expressions of quantities used in the calculation of the variances are dependent upon the unit of measure chosen. Consider the sales of bread or milk. The relative share of bread and milk will depend upon the physical unit which is used in the variance calculations. We can use for example, weight (kilograms of bread and gallons of milk) or volume (loaves of bread and bottles of milk). The proportions used in the sales mix and quantity calculations will differ according to the units of measure chosen if one product is heavily weight-intensive or the other volume-intensive. The consequences of this problem and methods of overcoming it are discussed by Peles (1986).

Gibson (1990) advocates that mix and quantity variances provide useful information only where there is an identifiable relationship between the products sold and these relationships are incorporated into the planning process. Where relationships between products are not expected the budgeted contribution for a period is derived from *separate* estimates of physical volumes and prices of each product. The mix which emerges from the combination of the separate estimates for each product does not constitute a planned mix. Gibson, therefore, argues that providing management with mix and quantity variances, where there is no identified relationship between the sales volume of individual products, is misleading because it incorrectly implies that a possible cause of the sales volume variance is a change in mix. The only possible 'causes' that require investigation are simply deviations from planned volumes for the individual products. Gibson provides the following examples of situations where identifiable relationships exist:

> The sale, by the firm of a number of similar products (differentiated by single characteristics such as size) where sales of individual products are *expected* to vary proportionally with total sales; the sale of complementary products (where increased sales of one product are *expected* to result in increased sales in another); the sale of product substitutes (where increased sales of one product are expected to result in decreased sales of another); and, the sale of heterogeneous products, the quantities of which are limited by factors of production (for example, where the sale of products with

lower contribution margins per limiting resource factor is made only if products with higher contribution margins cannot be sold).

Gibson identifies two possible situations where a planned relationship between the sales of products could be incorporated into the planning model. The first relates to where the total sales of individual products are expected to occur in a constant mix, such as different sizes of a particular product. In this situation management would be interested in how the volume variance has been affected by deviations from the planned mix. The second relates to situations where sales of products in a group are expected to vary in proportion to sales of a 'critical' product, such as where other products are complementary to, or substitutes for the 'critical' product.

By adopting Gibson's recommendation, and restricting the calculation of mix variances only to those situations where the relationship is planned Peles' criticism of combining physical units with dissimilar properties is overcome.

SUMMARY

In this chapter we have seen how quantity variances can be decomposed into mix and yield variances. In some production processes it is possible to vary the mix of raw materials and labour grades and thus affect the yield and cost per unit of output. A standard mix is determined which minimizes the cost per unit of output but which still meets quality requirements. By deviating from the standard mix operating managers can affect the yield and cost per unit of output. Yield and mix variances are, therefore, computed in order to provide an indication of the cost of deviating from the standard mix.

Where a company sells more than one product, the sales volume variance can be divided into a sales mix and a sales quantity (yield) variance. The mix variance measures the impact from the actual sales mix differing from the budgeted sales mix and the quantity variance measures the effect of changes in sales volume on total profits, assuming that the sales mix is held constant. Where industry sales statistics are available it is possible to divide the sales quantity variance into a component due to changes in market size and a component due to changes in market share.

The purpose of variance analysis is to identify and measure the separate elements (variances) that account for the difference between actual and planned outcomes. The objective is to provide *useful* information to managers. However, because of the mathematical relationships which exist, we must avoid the temptation of relying entirely on a mathematical methodology to explain the difference between actual and planned outcomes. If the analysis is based on variances derived solely from mathematical relationships there is a danger that the resulting variances will provide useless, or possibly misleading information. Reporting should be limited only to those variances which incorporate variables or relationships considered in the planning process. Mix and quantity variances provide useful information only in those situations where relationships are *expected* between inputs (or products) and these relationships are incorporated into the planning process.

NOTE

1. For the purpose of reconciling budgeted actual profits, sales margin variances should be measured in terms of contribution margins if profits are measured on a variable costing basis. Where profits are measured on an absorption costing basis sales variances should be expressed in terms of profit margins.

4

Variance Analysis: Alternative Approaches

The objective in the two previous chapters was to explain the variance computations presented in current management accounting textbooks. The term 'conventional variance analysis' will be used to refer to these variance computations. In this chapter we shall turn our attention to the criticisms of conventional variance analysis and consider some suggestions for providing a more meaningful approach to variance analysis. We begin by describing the ex post variance analysis model advocated by Demski.

EX-POST OPPORTUNITY COST VARIANCE ANALYSIS

The cost variances which we have calculated so far measured the cost of deviations of actual results from planned results for the output achieved. Sales variances were calculated by comparing budgeted and actual outcomes. The standards or plans were based on the conditions which were anticipated when the targets were set. However, Demski (1977) has argued that where conditions are different from those which were anticipated, actual performance should be compared with a standard which reflects these changed conditions. He states:

> The proper standard to be used in supplying variance information is a standard based on actual conditions – that is . . . those that would have been incorporated in the (original) plan if the actual conditions had been known in advance.

Demski uses the term *ex post* standard to refer to standards which would have been set if the actual conditions had been known in advance. The foregoing discussion is a description of the ex post variance approach advocated by Demski.

Demski uses the diagram reproduced in Figure 4.1 to illustrate the approach. It is assumed that the firm produces a single product and that the standard is the marginal cost curve. A profit maximizing firm, facing a marginal revenue curve of MR and a marginal cost curve of MC_0 will produce at output level X_0 and profit will be equal to area GDF.

Assume that there is an *unavoidable* shift in the marginal cost curve from MC_0 to MC_1. The profit maximizing firm will move from output level X_0 to output level X_1 and profit will be equal to area GBA. The resulting reduction in obtainable profit is area ABDF, but since the firm cannot now obtain the original cost curve MC_0, the firm is maximizing profit by producing at level X_1. Hence there is no foregoing opportunity associated with this event.

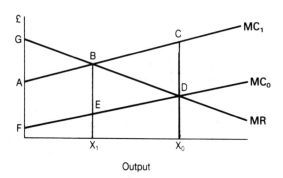

FIGURE 4.1 Ex post variance analysis

If, on the other hand, the firm remains at output level X_0, in response to the unavoidable increase from MC_0 to MC_1, it would incur a loss equal to area BCD in respect of the output in excess of the optimal level of X_1 (that is, the additional output of X_1 X_0). Area BCD thus represents the opportunity cost of the failure to move to the new optimum output level.

Let us now assume that the shift to MC_1 could have been avoided. The firm would maximize profit by remaining at X_0 and suppressing the avoidable increase in marginal cost. Area GDF would represent the maximum profits. If the firm does not suppress the increase and remains at X_0, it forgoes profit equal to area ABDF and incurs a loss equal to area BCD in respect of the output represented between points X_1 and X_0. The overall effect is that the firm forgoes obtainable profit represented by area ACDF. On the other hand, if the firm fails to suppress the increase in costs but adjusts its output level to X_1, it foregoes obtainable profits equal to area ABDF. In contrast the conventional variance analysis approach reports a variance equal to the difference between MC_1 and MC_0. If the firm remains at X_0, a variance equivalent to area ACDF will be reported whereas the reported variance will be ABEF if it moves to X_1. Demski provides the following summary of the total variances reported by the two approaches:

Shift in MC_0	Actual output	Optimum output	Conventional variance approach	Ex post opportunity cost
Avoidable	X_0	X_0	ACDF	ACDF
Avoidable	X_1	X_0	ABEF	ABDF
Unavoidable	X_0	X_1	ACDF	BCD
Unavoidable	X_1	X_1	ABEF	0

The conventional variance analysis approach does not consider the optimum adjustment to the changed conditions. It compares planned and actual results. You can see from Figure 4.1 that the total variance is represented by the difference between actual (MC_1) and standard results (MC_0) anticipated for the actual output produced. Demski also makes the point that if ex post standards are used, the conventional variance analysis model will only convey what performance should have been obtained for the output actually achieved. In other words, in Figure 4.1 the ex post standard would be MC_1, where the shift in MC_0 is unavoidable, and MC_0 where the shift is avoidable. Assuming that actual cost is identical to MC_1 a zero variance would be reported by the conventional variance analysis model where the shift from MC_0 to MC_1 is unavoidable. Irrespective of whether original or ex post standards are used, the conventional variance model reports divergencies between actual and standard cost for the output achieved. It does not, however, report what output *should* have been.

In contrast, the ex post approach model compares actual results with ex post optimum results, instead of with either ex post or ex ante standard results, for the output actually attained. The ex post model, therefore, reports the opportunities foregone from failing to respond to changes in conditions. By introducing into the analysis the optimal variation of the planned output, the proposed ex post system establishes a framework which indicates the best that might have been done, given the actual circumstances encountered during the period. The resulting opportunity cost variance should be subdivided, analysed by causes and traced to appropriate responsibility centres.

PLANNING AND OPERATIONAL VARIANCES

The ex post opportunity cost variance model illustrated by Demski (see Figure 4.1) assumes that marginal cost increases and marginal revenue declines, as output is expanded. Therefore any shifts in the marginal cost or marginal revenue curves will result in a change in the optimal output level, and foregone profits, if managements fails to adjust output to the new optimum level.

The cost and revenue functions presented in the accounting literature normally assume that variable cost and selling price are constant per unit of output within the relevant output range. In other words it is assumed that within this range marginal cost equals unit variable cost and marginal revenue equals selling price. The term 'relevant range' is used to refer to the range of output which the firm expects to be operating in the future. This range of output is represented by the output range between points A and B in Figure 4.2. Within the relevant range, total fixed costs are also assumed to be constant. Outside this range it is generally assumed that variable cost per unit may increase because the firm is no longer operating within the most efficient production range.

Our objective here is not to discuss the validity of these assumptions. Instead, we shall illustrate the ex post variance analysis approach taking these assumptions as given. In Figure 4.2 MC_0 represents the marginal cost curve based on standard performance anticipated when the targets were set. Assume there is an unavoidable shift in the marginal cost curve from MC_0 to MC_1 and that MC_2 represents the actual marginal cost for the period. We shall also assume that selling price per unit is constant. Therefore marginal revenue will be equivalent to the selling price. The planned output for the company is OB. You can see that within the relevant output range the marginal revenue and marginal cost curve curves are assumed to be constant. Therefore the marginal revenue and marginal cost curves do not intersect and optimal output will not be affected by shifts in the marginal cost or marginal revenue curves.[1]

Outside the relevant output range the MC curve would eventually increase because of diminishing returns to scale. The

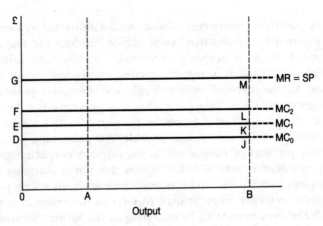

FIGURE 4.2 Planning and operating variances

MR curve would also decline as the selling price is reduced in order to increase demand. Hence the MR and MC curves would intersect. We shall, however, assume that the firm plans to operate within the relevant output range where MR and MC curves are assumed to be constant.

The conventional approach to standard costing compares actual cost (MC_2) with the standard cost envisaged when the targets were set (MC_0). Assuming that actual output is equal to the budgeted output of OB, a variance equivalent to area DFLJ would be reported. However, it is inappropriate to compare actual cost with the standard cost envisaged when the targets were set. Instead, actual performance should be compared with the ex post standard (MC_1) which reflects the actual circumstances encountered during the period. A variance equal to area EFLK would be reported. The unavoidable shift from MC_0 to MC_1 represents an uncontrollable planning variance arising from a change in the environment. This variance is represented by area DEKJ. The ex post variance analysis approach, therefore, analyses variances according to the following causes:

1. Operational controllable variances arising from efficiencies or inefficiencies and represented by the differences between the actual results and ex post target performance.
2. Planning uncontrollable variances arising from the differences between the original planned performance and the ex post revised planned performance. Planning variances, therefore, reflect the incorrectness of the original plans and standards arising from changes in the environment. They can provide a useful check on forecasting skills and also provide helpful feedback information on any required revisions to the original plans.

Note that in Figure 4.2 we have assumed that actual selling price and sales volume is equal to the ex ante and ex post planned selling price and sales volume thus resulting in zero sales variances. We shall focus on sales variances, adopting an ex post approach, later in this chapter. Bromwich (1988) has illustrated the potential practical applications of the ex post variance analysis. The foregoing discussion describes the approach illustrated by Bromwich.

Price variances

The traditional material price variances may be of little use for appraising the performance of the purchasing officer as it fails to distinguish between price changes due to market forces beyond his control and changes due to efficiencies or inefficiencies in buying. Consider Example 4.1.

EXAMPLE 4.1

The standard cost per unit for a raw material was estimated to be £6 per unit. The general market price at the time of purchase was £6.30 per unit and the actual price paid was £6.25 per unit. 10,000 units of the raw material were purchased during the period.

The conventional material price variance is £2,500 adverse (10,000 units at 25p). This variance, however, consists of an adverse planning variance of £3,000, which shows how the market price differed from that previously assumed, and a favourable purchasing efficiency (operational) variance of £500. The planning variance is calculated as follows:

Purchasing planning variance:
$$= \text{(Original target price} - \text{General market price}$$
$$\text{at time of purchase)} \times \text{Quantity purchased}$$
$$= (£6 - £6.30) \times 10,000$$
$$= £3,000A$$

The planning variance is not controllable but it provides useful feedback information on how successful purchasing managers are in forecasting material prices, thus helping them to improve their future estimates of material prices. Purchase planning price variances also play a major role in assessing whether price movements necessitate a change in existing plans, such as increasing selling prices, or changing production methods.

The efficiency of the purchasing department is assessed by a purchasing efficiency variance. This variance measures the purchasing department's efficiency for the conditions that actually prevailed and is calculated as follows:

Purchasing efficiency variance:

$$= \text{(General market price} - \text{actual price paid)} \times \text{Quantity purchased}$$
$$= (£6.30 - £6.25) \times 10,000$$
$$= £500F$$

Comparing the actual price paid with the best available estimate of the market price prevailing at the time of actual purchase provides an indication of the buyer's ability to 'beat the market'.

In some situations the buyer might attempt to 'beat the market' by engaging in speculative purchasing and buying quantities in excess of the normal economic purchasing quantity in order to avoid anticipated price increases. In this situation we should modify our analysis and calculate the purchasing efficiency variance at the point of usage rather than the point of purchase. Consider the situation outlined in Example 4.2.

EXAMPLE 4.2

The standard cost of a raw material is £5 per unit. The general market price at the time of purchase was £6 per unit and the actual price paid was also £6 per unit. 5,000 units of raw material were purchased during the period. This purchase represented an advance purchase in excess of immediate requirements in order to avoid a predicted price increase. Normally the materials are purchased at the point when they are required for production purposes. The predicted and general market prices for the later period (in which the materials would otherwise have been purchased) were £8 and £7.50 respectively.

If we adopt the approach illustrated in Example 4.1 an adverse material planning price variance of £5,000 and a zero purchasing efficiency would be reported. This information is not particularly useful in terms of appraising the performance of the purchasing department, or providing feedback to purchasing management on speculative forward purchasing decisions. In this situation the purchasing efficiency variance is determined by the difference between the general market price of £7.50 applying in the later period (in which these items would otherwise have been purchased) and the actual price paid for the materials of £6. A favourable variance of £7,500 (5,000 × £1.50) would, therefore, be reported.

In order to measure the profitability of such speculative activities the stock holding costs incurred on the purchase cost of £30,000 should be deducted from the £7,500 variance. By comparing the buyer's predicted purchase price of £8 with the general market price (£7.50) applying in the later period the buyer's forecasting success can also be measured.

The above approach illustrates that for control and performance measurement purposes, variance analysis should be related to the economic facts and take into account opportunities available. It is important that variance calculations should not be restricted to the rigorous application of standard formulae which is applied to *all* situations. A flexible approach should be adopted which aims to show how well a manager has performed in the prevailing circumstances and also provides useful feedback information which helps managers to improve future performance.

You should note that for financial accounting purposes production is costed at standard cost and the differences between standard and actual costs are diverted to variance accounts, and charged as an expense to the current accounting period. Therefore, in order to meet financial accounting requirements, the conventional price variance of £5,000 must be reported in respect of Example 4.2. For management accounting purposes, however, the success of speculative purchasing should be measured and a favourable purchasing efficiency variance of £7,500 reported. It is important that variances which are required for financial accounting purposes should not dictate the variances which are reported for management accounting purposes.

Material usage variances

This variance is less likely than the price variance to be affected by uncontrollable changes in the firm's environment. Such changes can, however, affect the material usage variance. For example, materials may be in short supply and it may be necessary to purchase inferior substitute materials. Alternatively, labour of a poorer quality than expected may be used, owing to shortages of skilled workers. In these situations material usage variances should be based on a comparison of actual usage with an adjusted standard which takes account of the change in the firm's environment. The difference between the original standard and the adjusted standard represents an uncontrollable planning variance. Example 4.3 illustrates the approach:

EXAMPLE 4.3

The standard quantity of materials per unit of production for a product is 10 kg. Actual production for the period was 500 units and actual material usage was 5,400 kg. The standard cost per kg of materials was £2. Because of a shortage of skilled labour it has been necessary to use unskilled labour and it is estimated that this will increase the material usage by 10%.

The conventional analysis would report an adverse material usage variance of £800 (400 kg at £2) but this is misleading if all or part of this variance is due to uncontrollable environmental changes. When the standard is adjusted to take into account the changed conditions, the standard quantity is 11 kg per unit which gives a *revised* standard of 5,500 kg for an output of 500 units. The difference between this revised standard and the original standard quantity of 5,000 kg (500 units at 10 kg per unit) represents the **uncontrollable planning variance** due to environmental changes. The uncontrollable planning variance is therefore £1,000 adverse and is calculated as follows:

(Original standard quantity − Revised standard quantity) × Standard price
= (5,000 − 5,500) × £2

The revised **controllable usage variance** is the difference between the standard quantity of 5,500 kg based on the revised standard usage, and the actual usage of 5,400 kg. Hence the controllable usage variance will be £200 favourable. The conventional material usage variance is £800 whereas the ex post variance analysis separates this into an uncontrollable adverse planning variance of £1,000 and a revised favourable controllable usage variance of £200. This approach produces variance calculations which provide a truer representation of a manager's performance and avoids any uncontrollable elements being included in the material usage variance.

Mix variances

In the previous chapter we noted that where it was possible to combine two or more raw materials a standard mix should be established which specifies the optimal mix of materials required to produce a specified number of units of output. The costs of the different mixes are estimated and a standard mix is determined based on the mix of materials which minimizes the cost per unit of output but still meets the quality requirements. Mix and yield variances are calculated in order to indicate the cost of deviating from the standard mix.

The optimal mix and yield will be altered by any changes in the relative input prices of materials. In this situation the mix and yield variance should be computed by comparing the actual mix and yield with the ex post optimum. The conventional mix variance compares the actual mix with the ex ante mix, which is no longer optimal, and prices the difference at standard cost. It does not, therefore, provide any indication to operating managers as to when it would be profitable to deviate from the original standard mix. Consider the situation outlined in Example 4.4:

EXAMPLE 4.4

The standard mix for producing 9 gallons of product A is as follows:

6 gallons of material X at £6 per gallon	£36
4 gallons of material Y at £7 per gallon	£28
	£64

A standard loss of 10% of input is expected to occur. Actual input was:

60,000 gallons of material X at £7.20 per gallon	£432,000
40,000 gallons of material Y at £6.80 per gallon	£272,000
	£704,000

Because of the relative changes in market prices the revised optimum standard mix is:

4 gallons of material X at £7.20 per gallon	£28.80
6 gallons of material Y at £6.80 per gallon	£40.80
	£69.60

The standard loss is expected to remain at 10% of input. The actual prices paid for the materials were identical to the general market prices. Actual output for the period was 92,700 gallons of product A.

The conventional variance analysis would report the following variances:

	£	£
Price variances: Material X (60,000 × £1.20)	72,000A	
Material Y (40,000 × £0.20)	8,000F	
		64,000A
Yield variance [92,700 − (0.9 × 100,000)] × £64/9		19,200F
Mix variance		Nil
Total material variance		44,800A

You will recall from Chapter 3 that the yield variance is calculated by multiplying the excess yield by the standard cost per unit of *output* (£64/9). The actual material input is in accordance with the standard mix (60% of X and 40% of Y) and a zero mix variance is thus reported. The feedback information from this variance does not, therefore, indicate that it would be profitable to deviate from the standard mix.

Let us now calculate the ex post mix and yield variances:
Actual usage in ex post standard proportions:

X = 40,000 gallons at £7.20	£288,000
Y = 60,000 gallons at £6.80	£408,000
	£696,000

Actual usage in actual proportions:

X = 60,000 gallons at £7.20		£432,000
Y = 40,000 gallons at £6.80		£272,000
		£704,000
Mix variance		£8,000A

Note that the mix variance is priced at ex post market prices and not the original standard prices.

You can see that the ex post mix variance signals to the operating manager the potential gains to be made from altering the materials input mix. In those situations where it is unreasonable to expect the operating manager to adjust the actual mix to the ex post target mix the mix variance should be regarded as a planning variance. On the other hand, where operating managers are expected to respond to relative price changes, deviations from the ex post mix represent a failure to implement the ex post standard and should thus be regarded as controllable appraisal variances.

Where the general market price is different from the standard price, usage variances should be priced at the ex post standard price and not the original standard price. Therefore, the yield variance should be priced at the ex post standard cost per unit of output (that is, £69.60/9 gallons). A favourable yield variance of £20,880 (2,700 × £69.60/9) would, therefore, be reported. In order to calculate the planning variance we must compare the original standard with the ex post standard for the actual output of 92,700 gallons.[2] For an output of 92,700 gallons the planned input is 103,000 gallons (92,700 × 10/9). The calculation of the original and ex post standards is as follows:

Original plan/standard:

61,800 (60%) gallons of X at £6 per gallon		£370,800
41,200 (40%) gallons of Y at £7 per gallon		£288,400
		£659,200

Revised plan/standard:

41,200 (40%) gallons of X at £7.20 per gallon		£296,640
61,800 (60%) gallons of Y at £6.80 per gallon		£420,240
		£716,880
Planning variance		£57,680

The ex post variance analysis would, therefore, report the following variances:

	£
Mix variance	8,000A
Yield variance	20,880F
Planning variance	57,680A
Total variance	44,800A

Let us now assume that the current market prices are £6 for material X and £7 for material Y, the same as the standard prices. In this situation the price changes are controllable and the price variances should be calculated by comparing the actual prices with the original/ex post standard prices. A total adverse price variance of £64,000 would, therefore, be reported. The actual prices paid for the materials no longer represent ex post targets. Assuming that the materials have already been purchased, and the standard prices equal to the current market prices, there would be no gains to be made from altering the standard mix.[3] Consequently the ex post mix would be equal to the original standard mix and a zero mix variance would be reported. In other words, where the general market price remains unchanged and the price variances represent deviations from the general market price, the ex post variances will, in most situations, be identical to the conventional variances.

Labour variances

The criticisms which we have identified for the material variances are also applicable to the labour variances. For example, the labour efficiency and wage rate variances should be adjusted to reflect changes in the environmental conditions which prevailed during the period. A situation where this might occur is when unskilled labour is substituted for skilled labour because of conditions in the labour market. It is necessary in these circumstances to adjust the standard and separate the labour efficiency and wage rate variances into the following components:

(A) An uncontrollable planning variance due to environmental changes;

(B) A controllable efficiency and wage rate variance.

The variances should be calculated in a similar manner to that described for material variances.

Sales variances

The conventional sales volume variance reports the difference between actual and budgeted sales priced at the budgeted contribution per unit. This variance merely indicates whether sales volume is greater or less than expected. It does not indicate how well sales management has performed. In order to appraise the performance of sales management actual sales volume should be compared with an ex post estimate which reflects the market conditions prevailing during the period.

Consider a situation where the budgeted sales are 100,000 units at a standard contribution of £100 per unit. Assume that actual sales are 110,000 units and that actual selling price is identical to the budgeted selling price. The conventional approach would report a favourable sales volume variance of £1m (10,000 units at £100 contribution per unit). However, the market size was greater than expected and, if the company had attained its target market share for the period, sales volume should have been 120,000 units. In other words the ex post standard sales volume is 120,000 units. Actual sales volume is 10,000 units less than would have been expected after the circumstances prevailing during the period are taken into account. The ex post variance approach would, therefore, report an adverse sales volume appraisal variance of £1m. Conversely if the total market demand had fallen because of reasons outside the control of sales management, actual sales volume would be assessed against a more realistic lower standard.

The difference between the original budgeted sales volume of 100,000 units and the ex post budgeted sales volume of 120,000 units, priced at the budgeted contribution, represents the planning variance. A planning variance of £2m (20,000 units at a contribution of £100 per unit) would, therefore, be reported. The sum of the planning variance (£2m favourable) and the ex post sales volume variance (£1m adverse) equals the conventional sales volume variance.

The ex post approach provides an opportunity cost view of the performance of sales management by reporting a foregone contribution of £1m. The conventional approach reports a favourable performance whereas the ex post approach reports that sales management has underperformed by indicating the cost to the company of neglected opportunities. The conventional variance is irrelevant since it merely indicates whether or not sales management has beaten an obsolete target.

In our illustration we have assumed that actual selling price was equal to the budgeted selling price. A zero sales price variance would, therefore, be reported and the sales volume variance would be equal total sales margin variance. It is questionable whether separating the total sales margin variance into a volume and price variance provides any meaningful extra information. We noted in Chapter 3 that selling prices and sales volumes are inter-related and that the logical consequences of lower/higher selling prices are higher/lower sales volume. It is, therefore, recommended that only the total sales margin variance is reported. The variance should be separated into planning and appraisal elements using the following formulae:

Total sales margin variance (planning element)
Ex post budgeted sales volume
× (Ex post selling price − Standard cost)
less
Original budgeted sales volume
× (Budgeted selling price − Standard cost)

Total sales margin variance (Appraisal element):

Actual sales volume × (Actual selling price − Standard cost)
less
Ex post budgeted sales volume × (Ex post selling price − Standard cost)

The ex post budgeted sales volume for a particular product can be determined by estimating the total market sales volume for the period and then multiplying this estimate by the target percentage market share. Where industry statistics are published this calculation should be based on actual total sales volume.

Where a company markets several different product lines separate variances should be calculated for each product line. Mix variances should only be reported where there are identifiable relationships between the volumes of each product sold and these relationships are incorporated into the budgeting process.[4]

VARIANCE ANALYSIS AND THE OPPORTUNITY COST OF SCARCE RESOURCES

At the start of this chapter we focused on the ex post variance analysis model described by Demski. This model assumed a rising marginal cost and a declining marginal revenue curve. We noted that shifts in the marginal cost or marginal revenue curves arising from avoidable or unavoidable changes in costs or revenues resulted in changes in the optimal output level. The ex post variance analysis model recognizes such changes and incorporates any foregone profit, arising from a failure by management to move to the new optimum output level, in the variance calculations.

Next the ex post variance analysis approach was illustrated when the marginal cost and marginal revenue curves were constant within the relevant output range. We focused on situations where shifts in the marginal cost curve did not result in the curves intersecting.[5] Consequently the optimum output level remained unchanged and there was no foregone opportunity cost arising from a failure to achieve the optimal output level.

Single resource constraints

We shall now consider situations where production resources are scarce. In this situation any failure to use the scarce resources efficiently results in foregone profits which should be included in the appropriate variance analysis calculations. To keep things simple at this stage we shall assume that only one production resource is scarce and that the ex post standard is identical to the original standard. An overview of the analysis is illustrated in Figure 4.3.

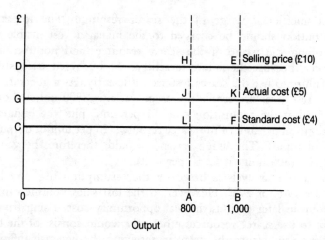

FIGURE 4.3 Variance analysis and the opportunity cost of scarce resources

Figure 4.3 illustrates a situation where a company uses a single resource which is restricted to 4,000 units. Each unit of output consumes 4 units of input of the resource. Therefore budgeted output is limited to 1,000 units (that is, OB in Figure 4.3). The budgeted cost per unit of output is £4 (4 units of input at £1 per unit) and the budgeted and actual selling price is £10 per unit of output. Budgeted total contribution for the period is, therefore, £6,000 (1,000 units at £6) and is indicated by area CDEF in the diagram. Assume that the actual consumption of the scarce resource is 5 units, instead of 4 units. Hence the actual cost per unit of output is £5 and is represented by the horizontal line GK. Maximum output will, therefore, be 800 units (4,000/5 units), represented by OA in the diagram, and actual profit will be £4,000 (800 units at an actual contribution of £5 per unit), indicated by area GDHJ. The difference between the budgeted and actual profit is £2,000 (represented by area HEFL plus area CGJL).

Conventional variance analysis would report an adverse usage cost variance of £800 (800 units × £1) equivalent to the area CGJL and an adverse sales volume variance of £1,200 (200 units at a contribution of £6 per unit) represented by area HEFL. However, the failure to achieve the budgeted optimum output level is due to the inefficient usage of the scarce resource. The foregone contribution should be charged to the manager responsible for controlling the usage of the scarce resource, and not the sales manager, because the failure to achieve the budgeted sales is due to a failure to use the scarce resource efficiently. As a general rule where resources are scarce the usage variance (800 units) should be priced at the acquisition cost (£1 per unit) plus the budgeted contribution per unit of the scarce resource (£6 per unit of output/4 units of input). The usage variance would, therefore, be valued at £2,000 (800 units at £2.50 per unit).

The above analysis is based on the assumption that any lost sales are lost for ever. However, if the lost sales volume can be made up in later periods the real opportunity cost arising from a failure to use scarce resources efficiently would consist of the lost interest arising from the delay in receiving the net cash inflows, and not the foregone contribution.

In order to provide a clearer understanding of the computation of variances when resources are scarce we shall compute the variances for the situation outlined in Example 4.5. An analysis of the variances and a reconciliation of the budgeted and actual profits is presented in Exhibit 4.1. Note that Example 4.5 has been designed so that *all the price variances are zero*. This will enable us to concentrate on the quantity variances. Let us now consider each of the columns in Exhibit 4.1.

EXAMPLE 4.5

ABC Ltd manufactures a single product, the standards of which are as follows:

		£
Standard per unit:		
Standard selling price		208
Less standard cost	£	
Material (10 kg at £4 per kg)	40	
Labour (8 hours at £8 per hour)	64	
*Variable overheads (8 hours at £3 per hour)	24	
		128
Standard contribution		80

*Variable overheads are assumed to vary with direct labour hours.
The following information relates to the previous month's activities:

	Budget	Actual
Production and sales	2,000 units	1,800 units
Direct materials	20,000 kg at £4 per kg	20,000 kg at £4 per kg
Direct labour	16,000 hours at £8 per hour	16,000 hours at £8 per hour
Variable overheads	£48,000	£44,400
Fixed overheads	£48,000	£48,000
Profit	£112,000	£74,000

The actual selling price was identical to the budgeted selling price and there were no opening or closing stocks during the period. Assume that direct labour is a variable cost.

You are required to calculate the variances and reconcile the budgeted and actual profit assuming:
1. Materials are restricted to 20,000 kg for the period and direct labour is not a scarce resource;
2. Labour hours are restricted to 16,000 hours for the period and materials are not a scarce resource;
3. There are no scarce production inputs.

EXHIBIT 4.1

Variance analysis for XYZ Ltd. (Example 4.5)

	(1) Conventional method £	(2) Scarce materials £	(3) Scarce labour hours £
Budgeted profit	112,000	112,000	112,000
Direct material usage variance	8,000A	24,000A	8,000A
Labour efficiency variance	12,800A	12,800A	28,800A
Variable overhead efficiency	1,200A	1,200A	1,200A
Sales margin volume	16,000A	Nil	Nil
Actual profit	74,000	74,000	74,000

Conventional method

The variances in column (1) are calculated according to the methods outlined in Chapter 2. You should turn back to Chapter 2 if you need to refresh your memory on the calculation of these variances.

Scarce materials

The material usage variance in column (2) is £24,000 adverse compared with £8,000 adverse using the conventional method. The conventional method values the 2,000 kg excess usage at the standard acquisition cost of £4 per unit.[6] However, because the materials are scarce the opportunity cost method illustrated in column (2) includes the lost contribution which arises from the excess usage because the scarce materials were not used efficiently. The product contribution is £80 and each unit produced requires 10 scarce kg of materials, giving a planned contribution of £8 per kg. The excess usage of 2,000 kg leads to a lost contribution of £16,000. This contribution is added to the acquisition cost for the excess materials giving a total variance of £24,000.

Because labour hours are not scarce the labour and variable overhead variances are identical to the conventional method. The computation of the sales margin volume variance, however, is different from the conventional method computation because the failure to achieve budgeted sales is due to a failure to use the scarce materials efficiently. Hence the cost should be charged to the responsible production manager and not the sales manager.

Scarce labour

Because it is assumed that materials are no longer scarce the materials usage variance in column (3) is identical to the conventional method calculation in column (1). Since labour hours are scarce the acquisition cost will not reflect the true economic cost for the labour efficiency variance. The conventional approach values the 1,600 excess hours at the standard acquisition cost of £8 per hour, but the opportunity cost method in column (3) adds the lost contribution from the excess usage of 1,600 scarce labour hours.[7] The product contribution is £80 and each unit produced requires 8 scarce labour hours, so each labour hour is planned to yield a £10 contribution. Thus the 1,600 excess labour hours lead to a £16,000 lost contribution. This lost contribution of £16,000 is added to the acquisition cost for the excess labour hours giving a variance of £28,800.

No scarce production inputs

Where there are no scarce production inputs the failure to achieve the budgeted sales volume is the responsibility of the sales manager. The lost sales volume of 200 units results in a lost contribution of £80 per unit, giving an adverse sales volume variance of £16,000. In this situation there is no lost contribution arising from the inefficient use of resources which are not scarce. Cost variances should, therefore, be priced at their standard acquisition cost. We can conclude that where production inputs are not scarce, and the ex post standards are identical to the original standards, variances should be reported adopting the conventional analysis illustrated in column (1).

Multiple resource constraints

In Example 4.5 we assumed that output was limited by one scarce resource and that a single product was produced. In practice several resources may be scarce and more than one product is likely to be manufactured. In this situation the optimum production programme must be determined using linear programming techniques. In addition to providing optimum output levels, the output from a linear programming model also provides details of the contribution obtained per unit of scarce resource. The terms shadow prices, opportunity cost and dual prices are used as alternative descriptions of the contribution per unit of scarce resource.

Let us assume that a company has used a linear programming model to derive an optimum production programme for a situation where materials, labour and machine hours are limited in supply. Assume that the model was developed using standard acquisition costs of £8 per labour hour, £4 per kg of materials and variable overheads of £2 per machine hour. Assume also that the opportunity costs (shadow prices) derived from the output of the model are:

Labour hours	£2.50 per labour hour
Materials	£1.50 per kg
Machine hours	Zero

The opportunity costs applying to labour hours and materials indicates that these resources will be fully utilized if the optimum production programme is implemented. In this situation any inefficient usage of these resources will result in a failure to attain the optimum output levels and a resulting loss in contribution. This lost contribution can be derived by including the opportunity cost per unit of scarce resource in the variance calculations. Consider a situation where the material usage variance is 500 kg in physical terms. The variance will be priced at the acquisition cost (£4) plus the lost contribution (opportunity cost) per unit of scarce resource (£1.50). Thus a material usage variance of £2,750 (500 kg at £5.50 per kg) will be reported. This variance includes an opportunity cost of £750 (500 kg at £1.50 per kg) which reflects the lost contribution from the lost output.

The zero opportunity cost for machine hours indicates that machine hours will not be fully utilized if the optimum production programme is implemented. Consequently inefficient usage of machine hours will not result in a loss of output or any loss in contribution. Therefore usage variances for resources which are not scarce will be priced at their standard acquisition costs. Hence the variable overhead variance will be priced at £2 per machine hour. Care should be taken in using opportunity costs derived from a linear programming model. Production constraints do not exist permanently and, therefore, opportunity costs cannot be regarded as permanent. Furthermore, the opportunity costs apply over a particular range of input levels. Outside this range the linear programming model must be amended to reflect the revised resource availability and new opportunity costs will emerge. Nevertheless, the same principles apply and the variances for scarce resources should be allocated with any additional or lost contribution arising from production efficiencies/inefficiencies. For a more detailed description of linear programming you should refer to Drury (1992, Chapter 22).

VARIABLE OVERHEAD VARIANCES

Variable overhead expenses can vary with direct labour hours of input, machine hours of input, number of units produced, quantity of material used and so on. Individual variable overhead items may vary with different volume measures. For example, indirect labour expenditure may vary with direct labour hours, whereas power to operate the machinery might vary with machine hours. In theory, separate variable overhead variances should be calculated for each individual item of overhead expenditure so that the variance computations take into account the fact that different items of expense vary with different volume bases.

Conventional variance analysis, however, generally assumes that *all* variable overheads are a function of a single volume measure, normally direct labour hours of input. In other words conventional variance analysis normally assumes that the budget is flexed on the basis of direct labour hours of input for *all* variable overhead items.

In an article first published in 1961, Solomons illustrated a more refined approach to variable overhead variance analysis which recognizes that variable overheads are a function of more than one volume measure. Solomons distinguishes between two types of variable overhead expenses:

1. Those that vary with volume of *output* such as manufacturing supplies and various material handling, maintenance and inspection costs.

2.   Those that vary with the number of hours of *input* such as indirect labour and heating and lighting.

Solomons illustrates how the variable overhead variances computations can be modified to reflect these two types of cost variabilities. The approach is illustrated in the situation outlined in Example 4.6.

EXAMPLE 4.6

The budgeted variable overheads for the period are £120,000. It is estimated that two thirds of the overheads vary with direct labour hours of input and the remaining overheads vary with output. Budgeted output is 10,000 units and two standard labour hours of input are required for each unit of output. Actual output for the period was 9,000 units, 19,000 direct labour hours were used and actual variable overhead expenditure was £118,000.

With the conventional approach variable overheads are assumed to vary with direct labour hours of input. Therefore the budgeted variable overhead rate will be £6 per direct labour hour (£120,000/10,000 units × 2 hours). The variance calculations are as follows:

Variable overhead expenditure variance:

Budgeted flexed variable overheads − Actual variable overheads incurred (19,000 hours × £6 = £114,000) − £118,000
= £4,000A

Variable overhead efficiency variance:

(Standard hours − Actual hours) × Standard variable overhead rate
[(9,000 units × 2 hours = 18,000) − 19,000] × £6
= £6,000A

These variances are calculated according to the methods outlined in Chapter 2. You should turn to pages 47–50 if you need to refresh your memory on the calculation of these variances.

We shall now re-calculate the variable overhead variances for Example 4.6 taking into account the fact that variable overheads vary with both the volume of output and direct labour hours of input. Two variable overhead rates are, therefore, calculated:

1. A variable overhead rate of £4 per direct labour hour of *input* [(2/3 × £120,000)/20,000 hours].
2. A variable overhead rate of £4 per unit of *output* [(1/3 × £120,000)/10,000)].

Note that where an organization produces more than one product, output would be expressed in terms of standard hours.[8] The variance calculations are as follows:

Variable overhead expenditure variance:

Budgeted flexed variable overheads − Actual variable overheads incurred

Input based	19,000 hours × £4	£76,000	
Output based	9,000 units × £4	£36,000	
		£112,000	− £118,000

= £6,000A

Variable overhead efficiency variance:

(Standard hours − Actual hours) × Standard variable overhead rate
(18,000   − 19,000)   × £4
= £4,000A

The approach adopted here recognizes that variable overheads are a function of two variables and, therefore, the budgeted is flexed on the basis of hours of input and units of output. In practice the expenditure variance will be examined item by item of expenditure rather than in terms of the total variance, as is done here.

The variable overhead efficiency variance arises because 1,000 excess hours of input were required. This will result in expenditure of £4,000 over and above the amount which should have been incurred for the actual output. The conventional approach prices the excess hours at £6 per hour whereas the more refined approach outlined here prices the excess hours at £4 per hour. This approach recognizes that only those variable overheads which vary with input hours will be affected by 1,000 excess hours of input being used.

Those variable overheads which vary with units of output will be unaffected by excess input hours or savings in input hours, as compared with the standard required to produce the actual output. Such expenses are determined by the actual output, not by the time it takes to produce it. The expenses linked to direct labour hours of input on the other hand, will be directly affected by excesses or savings in direct labour hours. It is these expenses, and these alone, which should enter into the variable overhead efficiency variance.

Note that both approaches report the same total variance (£10,000A). However, since the departmental manager is normally held accountable for the efficiency variance, but not the expenditure variance, care ought to be taken in determining the allocation of the total variance between the efficiency and expenditure subvariances.

The approach outlined here has illustrated how the variance analysis for variable overheads should be modified in order to reflect the fact that variable overheads are a function of two independent variables. It would be possible to incorporate more variables, such as machine hours and materials used, thus increasing the accuracy of the cost functions and the resulting variances. However, this would lead to greater complexity. Furthermore, it is costly to study the cost behaviour of each individual item of expense. It is generally assumed that for cost control purposes greater complexity is not worthwhile. Nevertheless it is important to recognize that conventional variable overhead variance analysis is based on the assumption that variable overheads vary with a single variable and that such an assumption is only an approximation of the true cost function. Care should, therefore, be exercised when interpreting overhead variances reported by the conventional method.

FIXED OVERHEAD VARIANCES

In Chapter 2 we noted that the fixed overhead variance could be divided into an expenditure variance and a volume variance. The volume variance can be further subdivided into a volume efficiency and volume capacity variance. The volume variance and the subvariances are computed for profit measurement purposes in order to meet financial accounting requirements. These variances have little economic significance for management and should not be used for planning, appraisal or cost control purposes.

An adverse fixed overhead volume variance results from either not utilizing budgeted capacity due to not selling the budgeted quantity, or inefficiency in not producing the budgeted quantity within the standard time allowed. Both causes will be reported either as sales variances or direct cost efficiency variances to the responsible managers and little can be gained from reporting the volume variances.

Fixed overhead volume variance analysis treats fixed overhead as being variable with production by using fixed overhead absorption rates per unit of output in the volume variance calculations. This results in the calculation of a volume variance whenever actual production is different from the activity level used to establish the standard overhead rate. The value of this variance can be very misleading as total fixed overhead expenditure will not change because actual production was different from budgeted production. It is more meaningful to adopt the approach illustrated in Example 4.5 and ascertain whether sales or production were responsible for the actual output being different from the original or ex post budget. The variance, expressed in terms of lost contribution, should be charged to the appropriate responsibility centre.

SUMMARY

In this chapter we have described various approaches for overcoming the limitations of conventional variance analysis. Our starting point was the ex post variance analysis model advocated by Demski. This model assumed a rising marginal cost and a declining marginal revenue curve. Consequently any shifts in the marginal cost or marginal revenue curves resulted in a change in the optimal output level. The ex post variance analysis model recognizes such changes and incorporates any foregone profit arising from a failure by management to move to the new optimum output level in the variance calculations.

We then turned to situations where marginal revenue (MR) and marginal cost (MC) curves were constant. Under such circumstances any avoidable or unavoidable shifts in the MC or

120   *Standard Costing*

MR curves do not lead to changes in optimal output levels as long as MC is less than MR. Conventional variance computations were criticized on the grounds that they failed to distinguish between operational (appraisal) and planning variances. Illustrations were presented showing how the ex post approach could provide more meaningful variance analysis information for direct materials, labour and sales variances.

We noted that where production resources were scarce, the conventional variance analysis did not take into account any opportunity cost arising from a failure to utilize scarce resources efficiently. It was suggested that the opportunity cost could be incorporated into the variance computations by pricing usage variances at their acquisition cost plus the lost contribution per unit of scarce resource.

Conventional variable overhead variances generally assume that variable overheads are a function of direct labour hours of input. It was shown how the approach could be modified in order to reflect the fact that variable overheads are a function of more than one independent variable. Finally we noted that the fixed overhead volume variance was required for financial accounting purposes but was of little economic significance for planning, appraisal and cost control purposes.

Variances are computed for both financial and management accounting purposes. There is a danger that variances computed for financial accounting purposes may dictate the variances which are reported for management accounting purposes. For example, Johnson and Kaplan (1987) claim that external financial reporting conventions encourage a financial accounting mentality in many corporate executives and this has resulted in management accounting practices following, and becoming subservient to, financial accounting practices. In order to meet financial accounting requirements the differences between standard and actual costs must be recorded and charged as an expense to the current accounting period. Such an approach may be inappropriate for management accounting purposes since our objective is to compare actual outcomes with opportunities which were available during the period. Variance reporting should not be based on the rigorous application of standard formulae which is applied to *all* situations. A flexible approach should be adopted which aims to report variances which show how well a manager has performed in the prevailing circumstances and which also provide useful feedback information to help managers improve their future performance.

NOTES

1. It is assumed that OB represents maximum sales volume at the existing selling price and that any reduction in selling price in order to increase volume beyond OB will result in a decline in total profits. It is also assumed that any shifts in the MC and MR curves will not result in MC exceeding MR within the relevant output range.
2. The planning variance calculated here represents the combined price and usage planning variance.
3. In this situation material price variances would be controllable and any adverse variances ought to result in corrective action in order to ensure that any inefficiencies would not be repeated in the future. The current reported variances would, therefore, represent sunk costs which reflect abnormal costs over and above the normal target costs. In this situation it is questionable whether there is any point in altering the standard mix since it is assumed that future purchases would be at the current standard/market price.
4. For a discussion of those situations where it is appropriate to compute and report mix variances you should refer to pages 89–90 in Chapter 3.
5. It was also assumed that within the relevant output range any shifts in the MR or MC curves did not result in MC exceeding MR.
6. The standard quantity of materials for an actual output of 1,800 units is 18,000 kg and actual usage is 20,000 kg. Therefore excess usage is 2,000 kg.
7. For an output of 1,800 units, 14,400 direct labour hours should have been used but 16,000 actual hours were used. Consequently, 1,600 excess labour hours were required.
8. The variable overhead rate per unit of output expressed in standard hours is £2 [(1/3 × £120,000)/20,000 budgeted standard hours)]. The output based flexed variable overheads will be £36,000 (18,000 standard hours at £2), the same as the figure calculated when production is measured in units of output.

5

Variance Investigation Models

In Chapter 1 we noted that a standard costing system consists of (1) setting standards for each operation; (2) comparing actual with standard performance; (3) analysing and reporting variances arising from the difference between actual and standard performance and (4) investigating significant variances and taking appropriate corrective action.[1]

In the final stage of this process management must decide which variances should be investigated. Management could adopt a policy of investigating every reported variance. Such a policy would, however, be very expensive and time consuming and would lead to investigating some variances which would not result in improvements in operations even if the cause of the variance was determined. If, on the other hand, management do not investigate reported variances the control function would be ignored. The optimal policy lies somewhere between these two extremes. In other words, the objective is to investigate only those variances which yield benefits in excess of the cost of investigation.

The purpose of this chapter is to consider some of the cost variance investigation models which have been developed in the accounting literature. These models can be classified into the following categories.

1. Simple rule of thumb models based on arbitrary criteria such as investigating if the absolute size of a variance is greater than a certain amount or if the ratio of the variance to the total standard cost exceeds some predetermined percentage.
2. Statistical models which compute the probability that a given variance comes from an in control distribution but which does not take into account the costs and benefits of investigation.
3. Statistical decision models which take into account the cost and benefits of investigation.

To help us understand the variance investigation models we shall start by considering the reasons why actual performance might differ from standard performance.

TYPES OF VARIANCE

There are several reasons why actual performance might differ from standard performance. A variance may arise simply as a result of an error in measuring the actual outcome. A second cause relates to standards becoming out of date because of changes in production conditions. Thirdly, variances can result from efficient or inefficient operations. Finally, variances can be due to random or chance fluctuations for which no cause can be found.

Measurement errors

The recorded amounts for actual costs or actual usage may differ from the actual amounts. For example, labour hours for a particular operation may be incorrectly added up or indirect labour costs might be incorrectly classified as a direct labour cost. There is also a danger that managers might deliberately manipulate the data in order to report a more favourable picture of operations than actually exists. The measurements used as an input to the variance computations should, therefore, be objective and possibly subject to occasional audits. Unless an investigation leads to an improvement in the accuracy of the recording system it is unlikely that any benefits will be obtained where the cause is found to be due to measurement errors.

Out-of-date standards

Where frequent changes in prices of inputs occur there is a danger that standard prices may be out of date. Consequently any investigation of price variances will indicate a general change in market prices rather than any efficiencies or inefficiencies in acquiring the resources. Standards can also become out of date where operations are subject to frequent technological changes or fail to take into account learning curve effects. Investigation of variances falling into this category will provide feedback on the inaccuracy of the standards and highlight the need to update the standard. Where standards are revised it may be necessary to alter some of the firm's output or input decisions. Ideally standards ought to be frequently reviewed and, where appropriate, updated in order to minimize variances being reported which are due to standards being out of date.

Out-of-control operations

Variances may result from inefficient operations due to a failure to follow prescribed procedures, faulty machinery or human errors. Investigation of variances in this category should pinpoint the cause of the inefficiency and lead to corrective action to eliminate the inefficiency being repeated.

Random or uncontrollable factors

These factors exist when a particular process is performed by the same worker under the same conditions, yet performance varies. When no known cause is present to account for this variability, it is said to be due to random uncontrollable factors. A standard is determined from a series of observations of a particular operation. It is most unlikely that repeated observations of this operation will yield the same result even if the operation consists of the same worker repeating the same task under identical conditions. The correct approach is to choose a representative reading from these observations to determine a standard. Frequently, the representative reading which is chosen is the average or some other measure of central tendency. The important point to note is that one summary reading has been chosen to represent the standard when in reality a range of outcomes is possible when the process is *under control*. Any observation which differs from the chosen standard *when the process is under control* can be described as a random uncontrollable variation around the standard.

Any investigation of variances due to random uncontrollable factors will involve a cost and will not yield any benefits because no assignable cause for the variance is present. Furthermore, those variances arising from assignable causes (such as inaccurate data, out-of-date standards or out-of-control operations) do not necessarily warrant investigation. For example, such variances may only be worthy of investigation if the benefits expected from the investigation exceed the costs of searching for and correcting the sources of the variance.

Variances may, therefore, be due to the following causes:

1. Random uncontrollable factors when the operation is under control;
2. Assignable causes but the costs of investigation exceed the benefits;
3. Assignable causes but the benefits from investigation exceed the cost of investigation.

A perfect cost investigation model would investigate only those variances falling in the third category. A decision model for the investigation of variances is illustrated in Figure 5.1. Let us now consider some of the cost investigation models which have been advocated in the accounting literature.

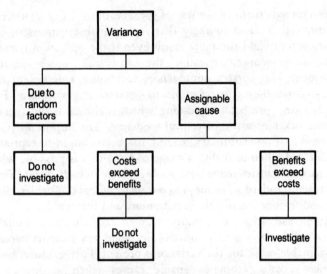

FIGURE 5.1 The variance investigation decision.

SIMPLE RULE OF THUMB COST INVESTIGATION MODELS

In many companies managers use simple models based on arbitrary criteria such as investigating if the absolute size of a variance is greater than a certain amount or if the variance exceeds the standard cost by some predetermined percentage (say 10%). For example, if the standard usage for a particular component was 10 kilos and the actual output for a period was 1,000 components then the variance would not be investigated if actual usage was between 9,000 and 11,000 kilos.

The advantages of using simple arbitrary rules are their simplicity and ease of implementation. There are, however, several disadvantages. Simple rule of thumb models do not adequately take into account the statistical significance of the reported variances or consider the costs and benefits of an investigation. For example, investigating all variances which exceed the standard cost by a fixed percentage can lead to investigating many variances of small amounts.

A further problem is that the variance investigation decision is based on a single observation, rather than monitoring the trend in the reported variances for a particular item of expense. The past history of reported variances is important because inefficiencies may tend to persist once they have crept into the process. There is a danger that the investigation process will not signal the need to investigate an out-of-control process where variances below the pre-set limit are consistently reported over several periods. Such variances can accumulate to significant values over several periods. On the other hand a decision to investigate, based on a single observation, can lead to investigating many variances arising from random uncontrollable factors which will not be repeated in future periods.

Some of these difficulties can be overcome by applying different percentages or amounts for different expense items as the basis for the investigation decision. For example, smaller percentages might be used as a signal to investigate key expense items and a higher percentage applied to less important items of expense. Nevertheless, such approaches still do not adequately take into account the statistical significance of the reported variances, or balance the cost and benefits of investigation. Instead, they rely on managerial judgement and intuition in selecting the 'cut-off' values.

STATISTICAL MODELS NOT INCORPORATING COSTS AND BENEFITS OF INVESTIGATION

A number of cost variance investigation models have been proposed in the accounting literature which determine the statistical probability that a variance comes from an in control distribution. An investigation is undertaken when the probability that an observation which comes from an in-control distribution falls below some arbitrarily determined probability level. The statistical models which we shall consider assume that two mutually exclusive states are possible. One state assumes that the system is 'in control' and a variance is simply due to random fluctuations around the expected outcome. The second possible state is that the system is in some way 'out-of-control' and corrective action can be taken to remedy the situation. We shall also initially assume that the 'in-control' state can be expressed in the form of a known probability distribution such as a normal distribution.

Determining probabilities

Consider a situation where the standard material usage for a particular operation has been derived from the average (that is, the expected value) of a series of past observations made under 'close' supervision to ensure they reflected operations under normal efficiency. The average usage is 10 kilos per unit of output. We shall assume that the actual observations were normally distributed with a standard deviation of 1 kg. Suppose that the actual material usage for a period was 12,000 kg and that output was 1,000 units. Thus average usage was 12 kg per unit of output. We can ascertain the probability of observing an average usage of 12 kg or more *when the process is under control* by applying normal distribution theory. An observation of an average usage of 12 kg per unit of output is two standard deviations from the expected value, where, for a normal distribution:

$$Z = \frac{\text{Actual usage (12 kg)} - \text{Expected usage (10 kg)}}{\text{Standard deviation (1 kg)}} = 2.0$$

A table of areas under the normal distribution indicates that there is a probability of 0.02275 that an observation from that distribution will occur at least two standard deviations above the mean. This is illustrated in Figure 5.2. The shaded area indicates that 2.275% of the area under the curve falls to the right of two standard deviations from the mean. Thus the probability of actual material usage per unit of output being 12 kg or more when the operation is under control is 2.275 per cent. It is very unlikely that the observation comes from a distribution with a mean of 10 kg and a standard deviation of 1 kg. In other words it is likely that this observation comes from another distribution and that the material usage for the period is out of control.

Where the standard is derived from a small number of observations we only have an estimate of the standard deviation,

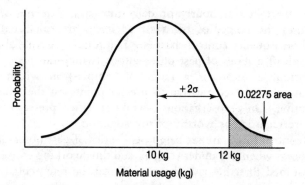

FIGURE 5.2 A normal probability distribution for the in-control process.

rather than the true standard deviation, and the deviation from the mean follows a t distribution rather than a normal distribution. The t distribution has more dispersion than the normal distribution so as to allow for the additional uncertainty that exists where an estimate is used instead of the true standard deviation. However, as the number of observations increases, to about 30, the values of a t distribution shown on a t table approach the values on a table for a normal distribution. Assume that the mean and the standard deviation were derived from 10 observations when the process was under control. The probability that a random variable having a t distribution with 9 degrees of freedom ($n - 1$) will exceed two standard deviations from the mean is still small, equal to approximately 0.025 (or 1 chance in 40).[2] Therefore, it is still likely that the observation comes from another distribution and thus the material usage for the period is out of control.

Statistical control charts

Variances can be monitored, by recording the number of standard deviations each observation is from the mean of the in-control distribution (10 kg in our illustration), on a statistical control chart. Statistical control charts are widely used as a quality control technique to test whether a batch of produced items is within pre-set tolerance limits. Usually samples from a particular production process are taken at hourly or daily intervals. The mean, and sometimes the range, of the sampled items are calculated and plotted on a quality control chart (see Figure 5.3). A control chart is a graph of a series of past observations (which can be a single observation, a mean or a range of samples) in which each observation is plotted relative to pre-set points on the expected distribution. Only observations beyond specified pre-set control limits are regarded as worthy of investigation.

The control limits are set based on a series of past observations of a process when it is under control, and thus working efficiently. It is assumed that the past observations can be represented by a normal distribution.

The past observations are used to estimate the population mean (μ) and the population standard deviation (σ). Assuming that the distribution of possible outcomes is normal then when the process is under control we would expect:

68.27% of the observations to fall within the range ± 1 from the mean.

95.45% of the observations to fall within the range ± 2 from the mean.

99.8% of the observations to fall within the range ± 3 from the mean.

Control limits are now set. For example, if control limits are set based on two standard deviations from the mean then this would indicate 4.55% (100% − 95.45%) of future observations would result from pure chance when the process is under control.

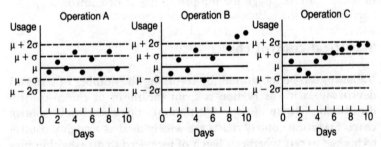

FIGURE 5.3 Statistical quality control charts.

Therefore there is a high probability that an observation outside the 2σ control limits is out of control.

Figure 5.3 shows three control charts with the outer horizontal lines representing a possible control limit of 2σ so that all observations outside this range are investigated. You will see that for operation A the process is deemed to be in control because all observations fall within the control limits. For operation B the last two observations suggest that the operation is out of control. Therefore both observations should be investigated. With operation C the observations would not prompt an investigation because all the observations are within the control limits. However, the last six observations show a steadily increasing usage in excess of the mean and the process may be out of control. Statistical procedures (called casum procedures) can also be used which consider the trend in recent usage as well as daily usage.

Statistical quality control is used mainly for quality control purposes but within a standard costing context statistical control charts can be used to monitor accounting variances. For example, labour efficiency and material usage variances could be computed for each operation and plotted on a control chart on an hourly or daily basis. This process would consist of sampling the output from an operation and plotting on the chart the mean usage of resources per unit for the sample output.

Statistical control techniques have been applied mainly to observations measured in physical terms such as number of product rejects, labour time and material usage. Plotting cost variances, instead of the variance measured in physical terms, is unlikely to provide any additional insight which will enable the variances to be better controlled *at the plant manager level*. Furthermore, the mean and the control limits will not be constant where standard prices are revised at frequent intervals. It would, therefore, be difficult to monitor trends, as illustrated in Figure 5.3 (operation C).

Plotting variances on control charts enables trends to be reported which can be easily interpreted by the human eye. In contrast, the statistical significance level approach, discussed earlier in this chapter, failed to incorporate prior observations into the statistical test. For example, assume that the dots in Figure 5.3 (operation C) represent weekly reported variances. We can see a pattern of steadily increasing accounting variances indicating that there is a shift away from the standard performance. However, the statistical significance level approach would be applied only to the latest observation and would not signal that the process was out of control.

Kaplan (1982) advocates that quality control charts should also be used by the accounting department to monitor key accounts. He suggests that twelve-month histories of key accounts could be presented in control chart format to enable managers to detect emerging problems faster than they could if only the data for the current and the previous month were presented in tabular form.

Limitations of statistical significance approaches

The statistical significance rules and quality control models which we have described suffer from a number of disadvantages. First, they do not take into account the cost of conducting an investigation or the benefits which might arise from making such an investigation. The costs and benefits of investigating individual variances will vary and the investigation should, therefore, incorporate these factors into the variance investigation decision. The second disadvantage is that prior observations are not taken into account, and only the most recent observation is used when computing the probability that the particular observation came from the 'in-control' distribution. We have noted that the previous history of each observation can indirectly be taken into account by monitoring the trend where the observations are plotted on statistical control charts. More complex techniques, however, have been developed which take into account the previous history by using the information from a series of observations to signal when a process has shifted away from a specified 'in-control' distribution. For a brief summary of these techniques, see Kaplan (1975).

Non-normal probabilities

Our discussion so far has presumed that the actual observations used to establish the standard performance can be represented by a normal distribution. There is no reason, however, why the analysis could not be modified to accommodate some other probability distribution. One could still compute the probability that a reported variance came from the specified distribution. The statistical significance rule can be applied to any probability distribution.

It is possible to make some probabilistic estimates even without making any assumption regarding the statistical distribution of the actual observations. We could use Chebyschev's inequality to determine the upper limit on the probability of a reported variance coming from the distribution of the outcomes which were used to establish the standard usage of materials. For Chebyschev's inequality it is assumed that the mean and standard deviation of the random variable is known but not the form of distribution. The inequality states that the probability of a random variable (x) deviating from its mean by more than K standard deviations is less than or equal to $1/K^2$, regardless of the shape of the distribution. In formula terms

$$\Pr\left|\frac{x - \mu}{\sigma} \geq K\right| \leq \frac{1}{K^2}$$

In our earlier example (see page 128) $\mu = 10$ kg and $\sigma = 1$ kg and actual average usage was 12 kg. This observation is two standard deviations from the mean. The probability of an observation deviating from its mean by more than two standard deviations is thus 0.25 ($1/2^2$). This is much higher than our earlier calculation of 0.025 obtained when an underlying normal distribution was used. Because of the high probabilities which arise from using Chebyschev's inequality the power of the statistical procedure is considerably reduced and its potential for practical use is, therefore, questionable.

DECISION MODELS WITH COSTS AND BENEFITS OF INVESTIGATION

The statistical decision models have been extended to incorporate the costs and benefits of investigation. A simple decision theory single period model for the investigation of variances was advocated by Bierman et al. (1977). The model assumes that two mutually exclusive states are possible. One state assumes that the system is 'in control' and a variance is simply due to a random fluctuation around the expected outcome. The second possible state is that the system is in some way 'out of control' and corrective action can be taken to remedy this situation. In other words it is assumed that if an investigation is undertaken when the process is 'out of control', the cause can be found and corrective action can always be taken to ensure that the process returns to its 'in-control' state. This assumption is more appropriate for controlling the quality of output from a production process but may not be appropriate when extended to the investigation of standard cost variances. For example, it does not capture situations where the investigation was signalled by measurement errors or the cause of the variance was due to out-of-date standards.

Costs and benefits of investigation

If the process is out of control, there is a benefit (B) associated with returning the process to its 'in-control' state. This benefit represents the cost saving which will arise through bringing the system back under control and thereby avoiding variances in future periods. However, if we do not investigate in this period, it is possible that an investigation may be undertaken next period. Therefore it is unlikely that the benefits will be equivalent to the savings for many periods in the future. Kaplan (1982) concludes that B should be defined as the expected one period benefit from operating in control rather than out of control, recognizing that this will underestimate the actual benefits.

A cost (C) will be incurred when an investigation is undertaken. This cost includes the manager's time spent on investigation, the cost of interrupting the production process, and the cost of correcting the process. We shall assume that the costs to correct an out-of-control process are negligible. This assumption ensures that the costs of an investigation which discovers that the process is 'out of control' are identical to the costs associated with finding that the process is 'in control'. However, the model can be easily modified to incorporate the incremental correction costs if the process is found to be out of control.

Determining the probabilities

To illustrate a one period model let us assume that the fixed cost of investigating the material usage variance in our earlier illustration (see page 128) is £100. Assume also that the estimated benefit (B) from investigating a variance and taking corrective action is £400. We can, therefore, develop a simple decision rule: investigate if the expected benefit is greater than the expected cost. Denoting P as the probability that the process is out of control, the expected benefit can be expressed as:

$$\text{Expected benefit} = PB + (1 - P).B$$
$$= PB + (1 - P).0$$
$$= PB$$

The probability that the system is in control is $(1 - P)$ and the benefit arising from investigating an 'in-control' situation is zero. Therefore PB represents the expected benefit of investigating a variance. Assuming that the cost of investigation (C) is known with certainty the decision rule is to investigate if:

$$PB > C \text{ or } P > C/B$$

In our example we should investigate if:

$$P < 100/400 = 0.25$$

The model requires an estimate of P, the probability that the process is out of control. Bierman et al. (1977) have suggested that the probabilities could be determined by computing the probability that a particular observation, such as a variance, comes from an 'in-control' distribution. They also assume that the in-control state can be expressed in the form of a known probability distribution such as a normal distribution. Consider our earlier example shown on page 128 where the expected usage based on actual observations when the process in control was 10 kg per unit of output with a standard deviation of 1 kg. We noted that the recorded actual average usage of 12 kg for a particular period exceeded the mean of the distribution by two standard deviations. We referred to a normal probability table to ascertain that the probability of an observation of 12 kg (or larger) was 0.02275 (2.275%).[3] The probability of the process being out of control is 1 minus the probability of being in control.[4] Thus:

$$P = 1 - 0.02275 = 0.97725$$

Recall that we ascertained that the variance should be investigated if the probability that the process is out of control is in excess of 0.25. The process should, therefore, be investigated.

Prior probabilities

The above approach has been criticized because it ignores prior information, such as the variances recorded in previous periods and subjective estimates by managers of the probabilities that an operation is in control or out of control. Various alternative approaches have been suggested for overcoming these limitations. These tend to be fairly complex but, to keep things simple, one of the least complex models based on an approach illustrated by Dyckman (1969) will be illustrated.

In order to illustrate this approach we shall make use of our earlier illustration where the expected value of material usage for an 'in-control' process is 10 kg per unit of output with a standard distribution of 1 kg. We assume again that there are only two mutually exclusive states, and that the alternative state represents the system out of control, in which case the expected outcome is a material usage of 13 kg per unit of output and the distribution also has a standard deviation of 1 kg. Thus, if the system goes out of control it moves directly from an in-control state with a mean of 10 kg to an out of control state with a mean of 13 kg.

In addition to information relating to the two distributions, we also need to estimate the probability that the system is in control before any variances are observed. This probability is known as 'the prior probability'. We shall assume that the prior probability that the process is in control is 0.90. Therefore the prior probability that the process is out of control is 0.10.

Bayes' theorem

Bayes' theorem can be used to combine the new information given by the variance and the prior probability that the system is in control. The theorem is a statistical technique for revising prior probabilities to reflect new information.

The two distributions described above are illustrated in Figure 5.4. Both distributions have a standard deviation of 1 kg, but the mean of the in-control distribution is 10 kg whereas the mean of the out of control distribution is 13 kg. The actual material usage of 12 kg is two standard deviations from the mean of the in-control distribution and one standard deviation from the out-of-control distribution. We are seeking here the *exact* probability of a particular observation rather than one greater than or less than the observation. In other words we are interested in the probability density function rather than the cumulative distribution function we use for interval estimates. Thus we refer to a table of the ordinates of a normal density function which gives the height of the normal distribution at each particular point (rather than the area under the curve). The probability of observing a value which is one standard deviation from the mean of the out-of-control distribution is 0.242 and the probability of a point being two standard deviations from the mean of the in control distribution is 0.054.

We can now use Bayes' theorem to determine the probabilities of the system being either in control or out of control, given that

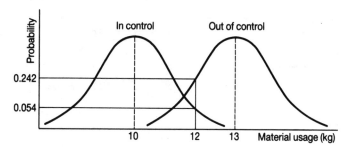

FIGURE 5.4 In control and out of control probability distributions.

a particular variance has been observed. To help you understand Bayes' theorem a decision tree relating to the illustration is shown in Figure 5.5. You will see from this diagram that the probability of an observation of 13 kg average usage, given that the process is in control is 0.0486 (0.90 × 0.054). The probability of observing 13 kg usage when the process is out of control is 0.0242 (0.10 × 0.242). Therefore the probability of an observation of 13 kg is 0.0728 (0.0486 + 0.0242). Thus the probability of the process being in control, given an observation of 13 kg is:

$$P \text{ (in control)} \mid P \text{ (observation of 13 kg)} = 0.0486/0.0728$$
$$= 0.67$$

Let us now use Bayes' theorem to calculate the probability of 0.67. In formula terms Bayes' theorem can be written as:

$$\Pr(A \mid B) = \frac{\Pr(B \mid A)\,\Pr(A)}{\Pr(B \mid A)\,\Pr(A) + \Pr(B \mid \overline{A})\,\Pr(\overline{A})}$$

The term $\Pr(A \mid B)$ is the probability of A occurring given that B has been observed. For the purpose of our illustration, A can be regarded as a particular state of the world (such as the system being in control) and B can be regarded as the observation of a particular variance. The term $\Pr(B \mid A)$ in the numerator relates to the probability of observing a particular variance of B, given that the system is in control multiplied by the prior probability

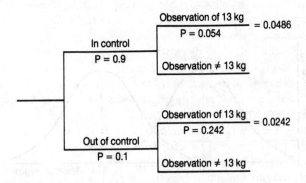

FIGURE 5.5 Decision tree to illustrate Bayes' theorem.

of A (Pr(A)), that the system is in control. The symbol $\overline{A}$ in the denominator means not the state of the world A. In other words 'the state of the world that the system is out of control'. Thus the last term in the denominator relates to the probability of observing a particular variance of B, given that the system is out of control multiplied by the prior probability of $\overline{A}$, that the system is out of control. Using Bayes' theorem the calculation is:

$$P \text{ (in control} \mid \text{observation of 13 kg)}$$
$$= \frac{0.054\,(0.9)}{0.054\,(0.9) + 0.242\,(0.10)}$$
$$= 0.67$$

Retaining our earlier assumption that the cost of investigating the variance is £100 and the estimated benefits are £400, we should investigate if the estimated probability that the process is out of control is in excess of 0.25. The above calculation indicates that the probability that the process is in control, given that an average usage of 13 kg has been observed, is 0.67. Thus the probability that the system is out of control, given the observation of 13 kg, is 0.33 (1 − 0.67). As 0.33 is in excess of 0.25 the variance should be investigated.

The problem of measuring costs and benefits

A major problem with decision theory models concerns the difficulty in determining the cost of investigation (C) and the benefits arising from the investigation (B). Note that B is defined as the present value of the costs which will be incurred if an investigation is not made now. In situations where the inefficiency will be repeated, there will be many opportunities in the future to correct the process, and the discounted future costs, assuming no future investigation, will be an overestimate of B. We have noted that Kaplan (1982) concludes that B should be defined as the expected one period benefit from operating in control rather than out of control, but recognizing that this will be an underestimate of the actual benefits. It is also assumed that when an out-of-control situation is discovered, action can be taken so that the process will be in control. In many situations the variance may have been caused by a permanent change in the process, such as a change in the production process or in raw material availability. In such instances the investigation will not exceed the expected benefit, since future operations will remain at the current cost level. The cost/benefit variance investigation model does not take such factors into account. Some benefits will be derived, however, since standards can be altered to reflect the permanent changes in the production process. This should lead to improvements in planning and control in future periods.

Problems also arise with determining the cost of investigating variances. The cost of an investigation will vary depending upon the cause of the variance. Some assignable causes will be detected before others, depending upon the ordering of the stages in the investigation procedure. If the variance is not due to an assignable cause, the cost of investigation will be higher because the investigation must eliminate all other causes before it can be established that the variance is not due to an assignable cause. Also, *additional* costs of carrying out the investigation may not be incurred as they may be carried out by existing staff at no extra cost to the organization. However, some opportunity cost is likely to be involved because of alternative work foregone while the investigation is being undertaken.

EMPIRICAL EVIDENCE

There is little evidence to indicate that the statistical variance investigation models presented in this chapter are used in practice. Lauderman and Schaeberle (1983) conducted a survey of the cost accounting practices of 100 large US companies and reported that:

72% of the firms informally investigated variances based on managerial judgement.

54% investigated variances which exceeded a given dollar amount.

43% investigated variances when the variance exceeds a given percentage of standard.

4% investigated variances based on statistical decision rules.

Similar findings have been reported by Puxty and Lyall (1989) and Williams (1986) relating to UK companies. A summary of their findings is presented in Exhibit 5.1. Both studies relied on postal questionnaire surveys but it is unclear whether or not the surveys included questions relating to the extent to which investigations were based on statistical significance rules. You can see from Exhibit 5.1 that firms use a combination of methods and that rule of thumb methods are extensively used.

SUMMARY

Several cost variance investigation models have been proposed in the accounting literature. These models vary considerably in terms of degree of sophistication. Variance investigation models can be classified into three categories:

1. Simple rule of thumb models which are based on arbitrary criteria and which do not take into account the statistical significance of reported variances.
2. Statistical models which compute the probability that a given observation comes from an in control distribution but which do not take into account the cost or benefits of investigation. An investigation is undertaken when the probability that an

---

EXHIBIT 5.1

UK surveys on variance investigation decision rules

	Puxty and Lyall %	Williams %
Investigation in all cases	9	22
Variance beyond a certain monetary figure	36	54
Variance beyond a certain percentage	26	32
Dependent on managerial judgement	81	35

    observation comes from an in control distribution falls below some arbitrarily determined probability level.
3.   Statistical decision models which incorporate the costs and benefits of investigation.

The statistical models can be further classified into single-period or multi-period models. With a single-period model the decision to investigate is based on a single observation whereas with a multi-period model the decision to investigate is based on some past sequence of observations.

    In this chapter some of the less complex models which have been proposed in the accounting literature have been described. These models do not capture all the factors which are likely to be involved in practice. For example, in most practical situations there will be more than two discrete states of the world. The shortcomings of simple models led to the development of more complex models which have attempted to be more realistic by getting closer to the reality of decision-making in practice. These models, however, have not been adopted in practice. A possible reason for this is that such models are too costly to implement as compared to their perceived benefits. For example, Magee (1976) performed a simulation study to evaluate the relative usefulness of simple and complex variance models. For a variety of assumptions on the costs and benefits of investigation and mixtures of in-control and out-of-control distributions the rule of investigating all deviations more than two standard deviations from the expected value worked almost as well, in terms of minimizing average costs, as the more complex models.

    Finally, it is important to note that the application of statistical techniques are more applicable to quantity variances, that is, labour and overhead efficiency and material usage variances. There is a fundamental difference between these variances and price variances. Efficiency cannot be predetermined in the same way as material prices and wage rates, first, because of the random variations inherent in the human element and, second, because the resulting non-uniformity is more pronounced. One does not expect actual results to be equal to standard where the human element is involved, as some variances may be expected to occur even when no assignable cause is present. For this reason statistical techniques are likely to be most useful when applied to the analysis of quantity variances.

NOTES

1. The process illustrated here refers to a standard costing system which is used for cost control purposes. We noted in Chapter 1 that a standard costing system is used for other purposes, besides cost control.
2. The probability 0.025 is derived from a t distribution table with 9 degrees of freedom.
3. It assumed that the actual observations used to establish the standard performance can be represented by a normal distribution. There is no reason, however, why the analysis could not be modified to accommodate the t distribution, illustrated earlier in this chapter, or some other probability distribution.
4. We assume here that all favourable variances are in control or do not warrant an investigation. If favourable variances two standard deviations from the mean are deemed to be out of control then the probability of observing a variance plus or minus two standard deviations from the mean is 0.0455 (0.02275 × 2). Consequently the probability that the process is out of control is 0.9545 (1 − 0.0455). The variance should still be investigated. Bierman et al. advocate a similar approach by stating that the probability of an event, given another event (in this case, an unfavourable variance) has already incurred, is based on considering only one half of the probability distribution. Therefore the probabilities derived from normal probability tables should be divided by 0.5. Thus:

$$0.02275/0.5 = 0.0455$$

6

Recording Standard Costs in the Accounts

Standard costs can be used for planning, control, motivation and decision-making purposes without being entered into the books. However, the incorporation of standard costs into the cost accounting system greatly simplifies the task of tracing costs for inventory valuation and saves a considerable amount of data processing time. Stock valuations based on standard costs may be included in externally published financial statements provided the standard costs used are current and attainable (Accounting Standards Committee, SSAP 9, 1988). Most companies which have established standard costs therefore incorporate them into their cost accounting recording system. The procedures for accumulating standard costs in the accounts and the disposition of standard cost variances are presented in this chapter.

ACCOUNTING ENTRIES FOR RECORDING STANDARD COSTS

Variations exist in the data accumulation methods that can be used for recording standard costs. In this chapter we shall illustrate a standard absorption costing system which values all stocks at standard cost, and all entries which are recorded in the inventory accounts will therefore be at *standard prices*. Any differences between standard costs and actual costs are debited or credited to variance accounts. Adverse variances will appear as debit balances as they are additional costs in excess of standard. Conversely, favourable variances will appear as credit balances. Only production variances are recorded and sales variances are not entered in the accounts.

Let us now consider the cost accounting records for Example 2.1 which was presented to Chapter 2. We shall assume that the company operates an integrated cost accounting system.[1] The variances recorded in the accounts will be those which we calculated in Chapter 2 and we need not therefore explain them again here, but if you cannot remember the variance calculations, please turn back now to Chapter 2 to refresh your memory. To keep things simple and to avoid confusion we will now repeat Example 2.1 and the reconciliation of budgeted and actual profits (Exhibit 2.5) for this example. The appropriate ledger entries are presented in Exhibit 6.1. Ledger and journal entries have been labelled with numbers from 1 to 13 to give you a clear understanding of each accounting entry.

EXAMPLE 2.1

Sigma manufacturing company produces a single product which is known as beta. The product requires a single operation and the standard cost for this operation is presented in the following standard cost card:

Standard cost card for product beta	
Direct materials:	£
4 kg of X at £2 per kg	8.00
2 kg of Y at £4 per kg	8.00
Direct labour (5 hours at £8 per hour)	40.00
Variable overheads (5 hours at £2 per direct labour hour)	10.00

Total standard variable cost		66.00
Standard contribution margin		44.00
Standard selling price		110.00

Sigma Ltd plan to produce 12,000 units of beta in the month of May and the budgeted costs based on the information contained in the standard cost card are as follows:

Budget based on the above standard costs and an output of 12,000 units

	£	£	£
Sales (12,000 units of sigma at £110 per unit)			1,320,000
Direct materials:			
X 48,000 kg at £2 per kg	96,000		
Y 24,000 kg at £4 per kg	96,000	192,000	
Direct labour (60,000 hours at £8 per hour)		480,000	
Variable overheads (60,000 hours at £2 per direct labour hour)		120,000	792,000
Budgeted contribution			528,000
Fixed overheads			240,000
Budgeted profit			288,000

Annual budgeted fixed overheads are £2,880,000 and are assumed to be incurred evenly throughout the year. The company uses a variable costing system for internal profit measurement purposes.

The actual results for May	£	£
Sales (11,000 units at £112)		1,232,000
Direct materials:		
X 45,000 kg at £2.10 per kg	94,500	
Y 24,000 kg at £3.80 per kg	91,200	
Direct labour (58,000 hours at £8.20 per hour)	475,600	
Variable overheads	114,000	775,300
Contribution		456,700
Fixed overheads		238,000
Profit		218,700

Manufacturing overheads are charged to production on the basis of direct labour hours. Actual production and sales for the period were 11,000 units.

EXHIBIT 2.5

Reconciliation of budgeted and actual profit for a standard absorption costing system

	£	£	£	£
Budgeted net profit				288,000
Sales variances:				
Sales margin price		22,000F		
Sales margin volume		24,000A	2,000A	
Direct cost variances:				
Material–Price: Material X	4,500A			
Material Y	4,800F	300F		
Usage: Material X	2,000A			
Material Y	8,000A	10,000A	9,700A	
Labour–Rate		11,600A		
Efficiency		24,000A	35,600A	
Manufacturing overhead variances:				
Fixed–Expenditure	2,000F			
Volume capacity	8,000A			
Volume efficiency	12,000A	18,000A		
Variable–Expenditure	2,000F			
Efficiency	6,000A	4,000A	22,000A	69,300A
Actual profit				218,7000

Purchase of materials

45,000 kg of raw material X at £2.10 per kg and 24,000 kg of raw material Y at £3.80 per kg were purchased. This gives a total purchase cost of £94,500 for X and £91,200 for Y. The standard prices were £2 per kg for X and £4 per kg for Y. The accounting entries for material X are:

(1) Dr Stores ledger control account (AQ × SP)   £90.000
(1) Dr Material price variance account   £4,500
   (1) Cr Creditor's control account (AQ × AP)   £94,500

You will see that the store ledger control account is debited with the standard price (SP) for the actual quantity purchased (AQ), and the actual price (AP) to be paid is credited to the creditor's control account. The difference is the material price variance. The accounting entries for material Y are:

(2) Dr Stores ledger control account (AQ × SP)   £96,000
    (2) Cr Material price variance account   £4,800
    (2) Cr Creditors (AQ × AP)   £91,200

Usage of materials

45,000 kg of X and 24,000 kg of Y were actually issued and the standard usage (SQ) was 44,000 and 22,000 kg at standard prices of £2 and £4. The accounting entries for material X are:

(3) Dr Work in progress (SQ × SP)   £88,000
(3) Dr Material usage variance   £2,000
    (3) Cr Stores ledger control account   £90,000
        (AQ × SP)

Work in progress is debited with the standard quantity of materials at the standard price and the stores ledger account is credited with the actual quantity issued at the standard price. The difference is the material usage variance. The accounting entries for material Y are:

(4) Dr Work in progress (SQ × SP)   £88,000
(4) Dr Material usage variance   £8,000
    (4) Cr Stores ledger control account
        (AQ × SP)   £96,000

Direct wages

The actual hours worked were 58,000 hours for the month. The standard hours produced were 55,000. The actual wage rate paid was £8.20 per hour, compared with a standard rate of £8 per hour. The actual wages cost is recorded in the same way in a standard costing system as in an actual costing system. The accounting entry for the actual wages paid is:

(5) Dr Wages control account   £475,600
    (5) Cr Wages accrued account   £475,600

The wages control account is then cleared as follows:

(6) Dr Work in progress (SQ × SP)	£440,000	
(6) Cr Wages control account		£440,000
(6) Dr Wage rate variance	£11,600	
(6) Dr Labour efficiency variance	£24,000	
(6) Cr Wages control account		£35,600

The wages control account is credited and the work in progress account is debited with the standard cost (that is, standard hours produced times the standard wage rate). The wage rate and labour efficiency variance accounts are debited as they are both adverse variances and account for the difference between the actual wages cost (recorded as a debit in the wages control account) and the standard wages cost (recorded as a credit in the wages control account).

Manufacturing overhead costs incurred

The actual manufacturing overhead incurred is £114,000 for variable overheads and £238,000 for fixed overheads. The accounting entries for actual overhead *incurred* are recorded in the same way in a standard costing system as in an actual costing system. That is:

(7) Dr Factory variable overhead control account	£114,000	
(7) Dr Factory fixed overhead control account	£238,000	
(7) Cr Expense creditors		£352,000

Absorption of manufacturing overheads and recording the variances

Work in progress is debited with the standard manufacturing overhead cost for the output produced. The standard overhead rates were £4 per standard hour for fixed overhead and £2 per standard hour for variable overheads. The actual output was 55,000 standard hours. The standard fixed overhead cost is therefore £220,000 (55,000 standard hours at £4 per hour) and the variable overhead cost is £110,000. The accounting entries for fixed overheads are:

(8) Dr Work in progress (SQ × SP)	£220,000	
(8) Dr Volume variance	£20,000	

    (8) Cr Factory fixed overhead control account   £240,000
(8) Dr Factory fixed overhead control account   £2,000
    (8) Cr Fixed overhead expenditure variance   £2,000

You will see that the debit of £220,000 to the work in progress account and the corresponding credit to the factory fixed overhead control account represents the standard fixed overhead cost of production. The difference between the debit entry of £238,000 in the factory fixed overhead control account in Exhibit 6.1 for the *actual* fixed overheads incurred, and the credit entry of £220,000 for the *standard* fixed overhead cost of production is the total fixed overhead variance, which consists of an adverse volume variance of £20,000 and a favourable expenditure variance of £2,000. This is recorded as a debit to the volume variance account and a credit to the expenditure variance account. The accounting entries for variable overheads are:

(9) Dr Work in progress account (SQ × SP)   £110,000
(9) Dr Variable overhead efficiency variance   £6,000
    (9) Cr Factory variable overhead control
        account   £116,000
(9) Dr Factory variable overhead control account   £2,000
    (9) Cr Variable overhead expenditure variance
        account   £2,000

The same principles apply with variable overheads. The debit to work in progress account and the corresponding credit to the factory variable overhead control account of £110,000 is the standard variable overhead cost of production. The difference between the debit entry of £114,000 in the factory variable overhead account in Exhibit 6.1 for the *actual* variable overheads incurred and the credit entry of £110,000 for the *standard* variable overhead cost of production is the total variable overhead variance, which consists of an adverse efficiency variance of £6,000 and a favourable expenditure variance of £2,000.

Completion of production

In Exhibit 6.1 the total amount which is recorded on the debit side of the work in progress account is £946,000. As there are no opening or closing stocks this represents the total standard cost of production for the period which consists of 11,000 units at £86 per unit. When the completed production is transferred from work in progress to finished goods stock the accounting entries will be as follows:

(10) Dr Finished stock account   £946,000
     (10) Cr Work in progress account   £946,000

Because there are no opening or closing stocks both the work in progress account and the stores ledger account will show a nil balance.

Sales

Sales variances are not recorded in the accounts, so actual sales of £1,232,000 for 11,000 units will be recorded as:

(11) Dr Debtors   £1,232,000
     (11) Cr Sales   £1,232,000

As all the production for the period has been sold there will be no closing stock of finished goods and the standard cost of production for the 11,000 units will be transferred from the finished goods account to the cost of sales account:

(12) Dr Cost of sales account   £946,000
     (12) Cr Finished goods account   £946,000

Finally, the cost of sales account and the variance accounts will be closed by transfer to the costing profit and loss account (the item labelled (13) in Exhibit 6.1). The balance of the costing profit and loss account will be the *actual* profit for the period.

Calculation of profit

To calculate the profit we must add the adverse variances and deduct the favourable variances from the standard cost of sales which is obtained from the cost of sales account. This calculation gives the actual production cost for the period which is then deducted from the actual sales to produce the actual profit for the period. The calculations are as follows:

	£	£	£
Sales			1,232,000
Less Standard cost of sales		946,000	
Plus Adverse variances:			
Material X price variance	4,500		
Material usage variance	10,000		
Wage rate variance	11,600		
Labour efficiency variance	24,000		
Volume variance	20,000		
Variable overhead efficiency			
variance	6,000	76,100	
		1,022,100	
Less favourable variances:			
Material B price variance	4,800		
Fixed overhead expenditure variance	2,000		
Variable overhead expenditure variance	2,000	8,800	
Actual cost of sales			1,013,300
Actual profit			218,700

ALTERNATIVE METHODS OF ACCOUNTING FOR MATERIALS

In Exhibit 6.1 we recorded the material price variance at the point when the materials were *received*. With this approach all transactions in the stores ledger control account are recorded at standard prices and the stores ledger cards for each individual item of material in stock are maintained in terms of physical quantities only. Some companies adopt an alternative method and record the materials at actual cost when received, and determine the price variance when the materials are *issued* to production. The accounting entries for transactions 1–4 are then as follows:

Purchase of material X	£	£
(1) Dr Stores ledger control account (AQ × AP)	94,500	
Cr Creditor's control account (AQ × AP)		94,500

Purchase of material Y		
(2) Dr Stores ledger control account (AQ × AP)	91,200	
Cr Creditors control account		91,200

EXHIBIT 6.1

Accounting entries for a standard absorption costing system

STORES LEDGER CONTROL ACCOUNT

	£		£
(1) Creditors (material X)	90,000	(3) Work in progress (material X)	88,000
(2) Creditors (material Y)	96,000	(3) Material usage variance (material X)	2,000
		(4) Work in progress (material Y)	88,000
		(4) Material usage variance (material Y)	8,000
	186,000		186,000

CREDITORS ACCOUNT

(2) Material price variance (material Y)	4,800	(1) Stores ledger control account (material X)	90,000
		(1) Material price variance (material X)	4,500
		(2) Stores ledger control account (material Y)	96,000

VARIANCE ACCOUNTS

(1) Creditors (material X)	4,500	(2) Creditors (material price Y)	4,800
(3) Stores ledger control (material X usage)	2,000	(8) Fixed factory overhead (expenditure)	2,000

EXHIBIT 6.1

Continued

(4) Stores ledger control (material Y usage)	8,000	(9) Variable factory overhead (expenditure)	2,000
(6) Wages control (wage rate)	11,600		8,800
(6) Wages control (lab. efficiency)	24,000		
(8) Fixed factory overhead (volume)	20,000	(13) Costing P & L A/c (bal.)	67,300
(9) Variable factory overhead (efficiency)	6,000		
	76,100		76,100

WORK IN PROGRESS ACCOUNT

(3) Stores ledger (material X)	88,000	(10) Finished goods stock account	946,000
(4) Stores ledger (material Y)	88,000		
(6) Wages control	440,000		
(8) Fixed factory overhead	220,000		
(9) Variable factory overhead	110,000		
	946,000		946,000

WAGES CONTROL ACCOUNT

(5) Wages accrued account	475,600	(6) WIP	440,000
		(6) Wage rate variance	11,600
		(6) Lab effc'y variance	24,000
	475,600		475,600

EXHIBIT 6.1

Continued

FIXED FACTORY OVERHEAD ACCOUNT

(7)	Expense creditors	238,000	(8) WIP	220,000
(8)	Expenditure variance	2,000	(8) Volume variance	20,000
		240,000		240,000

VARIABLE FACTORY OVERHEAD ACCOUNT

(7)	Expense creditors	114,000	(9) WIP	110,000
(9)	Expenditure	2,000	(9) Efficiency variance	6,000
		116,000		116,000

FINISHED GOODS STOCK ACCOUNT

(10)	WIP	946,000	(12) Cost of sales	946,000

COST OF SALES ACCOUNT

(13)	Finish goods stock	946,000	(13) Costing P & L A/c	946,000

COSTING P & L ACCOUNT

(12)	Cost of sales at standard cost	946,000	(11) Sales	1,232,000
(13)	Variance account (net variances)	67,300		
	Profit for period	218,700		
		1,232,000		1,232,000

Issues of material X

(3) Dr Work in progress account (SQ × SP)	88,000	
Dr Material price variance	4,500	
Dr Material usage variance	2,000	
Cr Stores ledger control account (AQ × AP)		94,500

Issues of material Y

(4) Dr work in progress account (SQ × SP)   88,000
     Dr Material usage variance   8,000
         Cr Material price variance   4,800
         Cr Stores ledger control account   91,200

After transactions 1–4 have been recorded the stores ledger control account would look like this:

STORES LEDGER CONTROL ACCOUNT

	£		£
(1) Creditors	94,500	(3) Work in progress	
(2) Creditors	91,200	(material X)	88,000
(4) Material price		(3) Material price	
variance		variance	
(material Y)	4,800	(material X)	4,500
		(3) Material usage	
		variance	
		(material X)	2,000
		(4) Work in progress	
		(material Y)	88,000
		(4) Material usage	
		variance	
		(material Y)	8,000
	190,500		190,500

In Example 2.1 actual purchases are identical to the actual materials issued during the period and the raw materials closing stocks are zero. Both approaches, therefore, allocate the net material price variance of £300 (£4,800 − £4,500) to the profit and loss for the current period. Let us now assume that transaction 4, relating to the issues of material Y, occurred in September instead of May. If you refer to Exhibit 6.1 you will see that the raw material closing stock at the end of May will be valued at £96,000 (AQ × SP). Compare this with the stock valuation for the alternative approach outlined above. Raw material closing stocks are valued at actual prices. Therefore the closing stock valuation would be £91,200 (AQ × AP) and the material price variance would not be recorded until the materials are issued in September. In contrast the material price variance would be recorded in May, at the time of receipt, with the method illustrated in Exhibit 6.1.

In Chapter 2 we noted that variances should be reported as quickly as possible so that any inefficiencies can be identified and remedial action taken. It was recommended that the material price variance ought to be extracted when materials are received and not when they are issued. Where the material price variances are recorded at the point of receipt raw material stocks are valued at standard cost, and subsidiary stock records for individual items of material are maintained in terms of physical quantities only. The value of raw materials stock may be obtained simply by multiplying the physical quantity of raw materials in stock by the standard price per unit. This saves a considerable amount of data processing time and avoids the need to record stocks on a first-in, first-out or average cost basis.

In contrast companies which record material price variances at the point of issue must maintain detailed records of receipts and issues at actual prices. This method is adopted so that stocks can be valued at actual, rather than standard cost. An approximation of stock valuations at actual cost, however, can be obtained by allocating the material price variance for the period between the raw materials stock and cost of goods sold. We shall illustrate this approach later in this chapter.

At this point you should be able to see that it is preferable to adopt the approach illustrated in Exhibit 6.1 and record all transactions in the stores ledger control account at standard prices. If standard prices do not provide a reasonable approximation to actual costs then an approximation of actual cost can be obtained by allocating the material price variance between cost of sales and the closing raw materials inventory.

DISPOSITION OF VARIANCES

At the end of an accounting period a decision must be made as to how the variances which have arisen during the period should be treated in the accounts. Variances may be disposed of in either of the following ways:

1. Adopt the method illustrated in Exhibit 6.1 and charge the variances as expenses to the period in which they arise. With this approach inventories are valued at standard cost.
2. Allocate the variances between inventories and cost of goods sold.

If standards are current and attainable then charging the total amount of the variances for the period to the profit and loss account is recommended as the variances are likely to represent efficiencies or inefficiencies. This approach is justified on the grounds that the cost of inefficient operations is not recoverable in the selling price, and should not therefore be deferred and included in the stock valuation, but should be charged to the period in which the inefficiency occurred.

Where standards are not current the second method can be used and variances allocated between inventories and cost of goods sold. The effect is to include with the cost of inventories that portion of the variance which is applicable to the stocks in inventory and thereby to arrive at the approximate actual cost of these stocks. In practice a company may treat different types of variances in different ways. Some may be written off in their entirety against the current period while others may be divided between inventories and cost of goods sold. For example, price variances are frequently not controllable by a firm because they can arise following changes in the external market prices. It can therefore be argued that those price variances which are unavoidable should be allocated between inventories and cost of goods sold.

To illustrate the method of allocating variances between inventories and cost of goods sold consider a situation where the percentages of cost elements in the inventories and cost of goods sold are as follows:

	Materials %	Labour %	Factory overhead %
Raw material stocks	20	–	–
Work in progress	10	15	20
Finished goods stocks	15	25	30
Cost of goods sold	55	60	50
	100	100	100

Assume that the following variances for a period are to be allocated between inventories and cost of goods sold:

	£
Material price	30,000
Wage rate	20,000
Overhead expenditure	10,000

The variances would be allocated as follows:

	Material price £	Wage rate £	Overhead expenditure £	Total £
Raw material stocks	6,000	nil	nil	6,000
Work in progress	3,000	3,000	2,000	8,000
Finished goods stocks	4,500	5,000	3,000	12,500
Cost of goods sold	16,500	12,000	5,000	33,500
	30,000	20,000	10,000	60,000

At the end of the period the above figures are allocated to the cost of sales and inventory accounts, but the subsidiary inventory accounts and records are not adjusted. At the beginning of the next period the inventory allocations are reversed (by crediting the inventory accounts and debiting the variance accounts) in order to return beginning inventories to standard costs. At the end of that period, the amounts reversed plus new variances are allocated in the same manner as before, based on the standard cost of ending inventory and cost of goods sold balances.

SUMMARY

This chapter has illustrated the procedure for accumulating standard costs and disposing of standard cost variances. Incorporating standard costs into the cost accounting system saves a considerable amount of data processing time by eliminating the need to trace actual costs to products for inventory valuation purposes. Where standard costs are formally recorded production is costed at standard cost, and the differences between standard and actual costs are diverted to variance accounts, and disposed of in total.

Variations exist in the data accumulation methods for recording standard costs. The illustration used in this chapter recorded all entries in inventory accounts at standard costs. With this method material price variances are recorded at the point of receipt. We contrasted this with an alternative method whereby the material price variance was recorded at the point where materials were issued to production. This method was not recommended because it resulted in a delay in reporting variances and required the maintenance of detailed records of receipts and issues at actual prices.

Two methods were described for disposing of the variances which have arisen during the period. With the first method inventories are stated at standard cost and variances are charged as expenses of the period in which they arise. This method is justified on the grounds that variances represent inefficiencies and avoidable waste not recoverable in the selling price. These variances should therefore be treated as period costs rather than being deferred and allocated to inventory accounts. This reasoning assumes that standards are current and attainable and, where appropriate, standards are revised to reflect any changes in external factors such as prices or changes in production methods.

With the second method variances are allocated between inventories and cost of goods sold thereby converting both inventories and cost of sales to approximate actual costs. This method is appropriate where standards are not current or the variances are the result of unavoidable price changes. Savings in data processing time are not therefore dependent on current and attainable standards being maintained.

NOTE

1. An integrated cost accounting system is a system in which the cost and financial accounts are combined in one set of accounts. An

alternative system where the cost and financial accounts are maintained independently is known as an interlocking accounting system. For an illustration of integrated and interlocking accounting procedures for an actual costing system (see Drury 1992, chapter 5).

7

Standard Costing in an Advanced Manufacturing Environment

In the 1980s advanced manufacturing technologies such as computer-aided design (CAD), computer numerically controlled (CNC) machines, flexible manufacturing systems (FMS) and just-in-time (JIT) manufacturing techniques dramatically changed the production processes of many companies throughout the world. Today, companies are becoming increasingly aware that excellence in manufacturing can provide a competitive weapon to compete in sophisticated world-wide markets.

In order to compete effectively, companies must be capable of manufacturing innovative products of high quality at a low cost and also provide a first-class customer service. At the same time they must have the flexibility to cope with short product life cycles, demands for greater product variety from more discriminating customers and increasing international competition.

World-class manufacturing companies have responded to these competitive demands by changing the production process in order to improve quality, reduce set-up times, increase manufacturing flexibility and lower the uncertainty of the overall production

162

process arising from restrictive work practices, erratic machine performance and the reliability of suppliers' deliveries. These companies, however, found that their existing management accounting systems did not support the objectives of automated manufacturing and JIT production techniques. It is therefore important that companies which invest in advanced manufacturing technologies (AMTs) take steps to ensure that their management accounting systems will lead to the performance needed in the new manufacturing environment. In order to understand the effect that AMTs and JIT manufacturing techniques will have on cost control and performance measurement systems (especially standard costing variance analysis), and how these systems must change to meet the requirements of the new manufacturing environment, we shall start by briefly outlining the major features of the new manufacturing environment.

ADVANCED MANUFACTURING TECHNOLOGIES AND JIT PRODUCTION SYSTEMS

Investment in AMTs dramatically changes cost behaviour patterns. Computer technicians, software engineers and programmers replace direct labour and variable costs disappear, except for purchases of materials and energy required to operate the equipment. More of a firm's costs become fixed (and sunk) and direct labour costs represent only a small percentage of total manufacturing cost. Overhead costs are a much higher fraction of total costs and consequently need to be understood and controlled much more carefully than in the past. These changes in cost structure have important implications for the future role of standard cost systems.

JIT manufacturing is best described as a philosophy of management dedicated to the elimination of waste and the constant pursuit of improvement. Waste is defined as anything that does not add customer perceived value to a product. The lead time involved in manufacturing and selling a product consists of process time, inspection time, move time, queue time and storage time. Of these five steps, only process time actually adds value to the product. All the other activities add cost but no value to the product and are thus deemed as non value added processes within the JIT philosophy.

According to Berliner and Brimson (1988) process time is less than 10% of total manufacturing lead time in many organizations in the USA. Therefore 90% of the manufacturing lead time associated with a product adds costs, but no value, to the product. By adopting a JIT philosophy and focusing on reducing lead times it is claimed that total costs can be significantly reduced.

The first stage in implementing JIT manufacturing techniques is to rearrange the factory floor away from a batch production functional layout towards a product layout using flow lines. With a functional plant layout products pass through a number of specialist departments which normally contain a group of similar machines. Products are processed in large batches so as to minimize the set-up times when machine settings are changed between processing batches of different products. Batches move via different and complex routes through the various departments, travelling over much of the factory floor before they are completed. Each process normally involves a considerable amount of waiting time. In addition much time is taken transporting items from one process to another. The consequences of this complex routing process are high work in progress levels and long manufacturing lead times.

The JIT solution is to reorganize the production process by grouping the products into families of similar products. All the products in a particular group will have similar production requirements and routings. Production is rearranged so that each product family is manufactured on a flow line. In a product line flow, specialist departments containing similar machines no longer exist. Instead, groups of dissimilar machines are organized into product family flow lines that function like an assembly line. For each product line the machines are placed close together in the order in which they are required by the group of products to be processed. Items in each product family can now move from process to process more easily thereby reducing work in progress and lead times. The aim is to produce products from start to finish without returning to the stock room.

JIT manufacturing aims to produce the right parts at the right time, only when they are needed, and only in the quantity needed. This philosophy has resulted in a 'pull' manufacturing system which means that parts move through the production system based on end-unit demand, focusing on maintaining a constant flow of components rather than batches of work in progress (WIP). JIT techniques aim to keep the materials moving in a continuous flow with no stoppages and no storage.

The 'pull' system is implemented by monitoring the consumption of parts at each operation stage and using various types of signalling systems to authorize production and movement of the part to the using location. The producing cell cannot run the parts until authorized to do so. This process can result in idle time in certain locations within the cell but JIT philosophy considers it is more beneficial to absorb short-run idle time rather than adding to inventory during these periods.

In a JIT environment the emphasis is on doing the job right the first time because a defective part disrupts the flow of production when all processes are operating with a minimal level of inventory. A company operating in a JIT environment becomes very aware of the fact that quality reduces costs rather than increasing them because of defects stopping the production line, thus creating rework and possibly resulting in a failure to meet delivery dates. By adopting new quality awareness programmes and implementing statistical process controls many JIT firms have decreased defect rates substantially, reduced inventories and enhanced the attributes of their products.

The JIT philosophy also extends to adopting JIT purchasing techniques whereby the delivery of materials immediately precedes their use. By arranging with suppliers for more frequent deliveries of smaller quantities, stocks can be cut to a minimum. Considerable savings in material handling expenses can be obtained by requiring suppliers to inspect materials before their delivery and guaranteeing their quality. This improved service is obtained by giving more business to fewer suppliers and placing long-term purchasing orders. Therefore the supplier has an assurance on long-term sales and can plan to meet this demand.

JIT requires a total commitment to excellence in every facet of the business. The ultimate aim advocated by the proponents of JIT is to achieve perfection which is defined as:

- Zero inventory.
- Zero defects.
- Batch sizes of one.
- A 100 per cent on-time delivery service.

It is questionable whether these ultimate aims of zero inventories and defects, and batch sizes of one, can be justified on economic grounds. Caution should be exercised. For example, any disruptions in the sources of supply, such as industrial action by the employees of the supplier firms or within the distribution transport system, could halt the whole production process of a JIT firm which maintains zero inventories. Consider how the power stations and the National Coal Board would have coped during the miners' strike if they had implemented a JIT zero stock philosophy. It is also most unlikely that batch sizes of one can be justified on economic grounds if set-up times are significant.

Policies relating to levels of inventories, defects and batch sizes should be based on an economic assessment, rather than always aiming for perfection. The costs and benefits of achieving perfection should be compared. It is unlikely that a policy of perfection will be appropriate in all circumstances. Nevertheless, adopting a JIT philosophy provides the potential for substantially reducing the level of waste in an organization.

Finally, you should note that JIT manufacturing techniques are not suitable for all organizations. JIT is most suited to an organization which produces a small range of high volume products processed through a number of stages. It is not suitable for companies which produce a wide range of low volume products.

LIMITATION OF STANDARD COSTING WITHIN AN ADVANCED MANUFACTURING ENVIRONMENT

Standard costing systems were developed to meet the needs of a traditional manufacturing environment which is drastically different from an AMT and JIT production environment. A number of writers are questioning the value of standard costing variance analysis in an AMT environment. The role of variance analysis in a mainly fixed cost manufacturing environment will have to be reviewed. If direct labour costs are mainly fixed and sunk, the reporting of direct labour variances is likely to be of little use for short-term operational cost control. Most of the overhead costs are unrelated to short-term changes in production volume. Variance analysis does not provide particularly useful information for cost control purposes where overhead spending is unrelated to production volume.

Volume-based variable overheads (e.g., energy costs for running the machines) are likely to represent only a small proportion of total manufacturing costs and to be a function of machine hours rather than direct labour hours. Such overheads, however, are likely to be pre-determined by the production technology and may not be controllable by operating managers. It may therefore be appropriate to report only direct material variances.

Material price variances

The reporting of material price variances may also be inappropriate where firms have adopted JIT purchasing techniques. If purchasing price variances are used to evaluate the performance of purchasing management it is likely that the purchasing manager will be motivated to focus entirely on obtaining materials at the lowest possible prices even if this results in:

- The use of many suppliers (all of them selected on the basis of price).
- Large quantity purchases thus resulting in higher inventories.
- Delivery of lower quality goods.
- Indifference to attaining on-time delivery.

JIT companies will wish to focus on performance measures which emphasize quality and reliability rather than material price variances which direct attention away from these key factors. The performance measurements must encompass all the factors important to the purchasing function, such as quality and reliability of suppliers, and not just price.

Failure to encourage continuous improvement

It is claimed that the concept of setting standards as targets is not consistent with a JIT philosophy of continuous improvement. When standards are set, a climate is created whereby the standards represent a target to be achieved and maintained, rather than a philosophy of constant improvement. The JIT philosophy requires that actual performance measures should be reported over time, rather than comparisons against a standard, so that the trend in performance can be monitored. Presenting performance measures over time communicates useful feedback information on the amount of rate of change in performance.

Performance measures motivate managers to maximize output

JIT manufacturing techniques aim to move orders through the factory in batches that are as small as possible based on a 'pull' production system. This process enables WIP and lead times to be minimized. However, most production and efficiency measures generally report declining efficiency if small batches are produced. This is because efficiency measures report output in relation to input and the input part of the equation normally includes an allowance for setting up the machinery. Managers are therefore encouraged to increase batch sizes rather than reduce them. The result is increased inventories, longer lead times and reduced customer responsiveness, all of which are contrary to the JIT philosophy. We have seen that JIT manufacturing aims to produce the right parts, at the right time and only when they are needed. This process can result in idle time in certain locations within the cell but the JIT philosophy considers it more beneficial to absorb short-run idle time rather than adding to inventory during these periods. Traditional manufacturing controls and performance measures, however, tend to place great emphasis on maximizing output. Workers are encouraged to maximize output even if this results in an increase in inventories and finance charges. Maximizing output, however, does not necessarily maximize long-term profitability.

The fixed overhead volume variance has been singled out as one of the major culprits responsible for encouraging managers to expand output. You will recall from Chapter 2 that the volume variance measures the under/over recovery of fixed overheads when stocks are valued on an absorption costing basis. With an absorption costing system favourable volume variances are reported whenever actual production exceeds budgeted production. Managers may therefore be motivated to increase inventories by expanding output.

In Chapter 2 we suggested that volume variances were inappropriate for cost control and performance appraisal purposes and should be computed only for stock valuation and profit measurement purposes. The under/over recovery of fixed overheads which is measured by the volume variance must be reported in order to meet the Statement of Standard Accounting Practice (SSAP 9), for external financial accounting requirements. Consequently even if a firm abandoned standard costing the under/over recovery of overheads must still be reported. It is therefore inappropriate to single out standard costing variance analysis as being responsible for encouraging excess production. However, according to Johnson and Kaplan (1987) external financial reporting conventions encourage a financial accounting mentality in many corporate executives and this has resulted in management accounting practices following, and becoming subservient to, financial accounting practices. It is therefore possible that fixed overhead volume variances are being incorrectly used by some companies for short-term operational control and performance appraisal purposes.

Over-emphasis on direct labour

Some writers have criticized standard costing on the grounds that it encourages too much attention to be focused on reporting variances related to direct labour. Surveys of firms operating in an advanced manufacturing environment indicate that labour costs range between 5% and 15% of total cost. Nevertheless, a survey by Computer-aided Manufacturing International (CAMI) reported that many firms recovered fixed overheads on a direct labour-hour basis. To reduce their allocated costs managers are motivated to reduce direct labour hours since this is the basis on which all other costs are attached to cost centres. This process overstates the importance of direct labour and directs attention away from controlling escalating overhead costs. This overemphasis on direct labour arises, not from any inadequacies of standard costing, but from the faulty application of standard costing by incorrectly using variances which have been computed for financial accounting for short-term operational cost control and performance appraisal purposes.

Failure to report key success measures

Management accounting control and performance reporting systems have also been criticized because they fail to report on such issues as quality, reliability, lead times, flexibility in responding to customer requirements and customer satisfaction. None of these issues is directly measured by traditional management accounting reports, despite the fact that they represent the major strategic manufacturing goals of world class manufacturing companies. Management accounting reports tend to focus mainly on reporting variances from standard cost. Consequently there is a danger that managers and employees are motivated to focus exclusively on cost and ignore other important marketing, management and strategic considerations.

Delayed feedback reporting

A further criticism of variance reporting is that performance reports arrive too late to be of value in controlling production operations. Performance reports are normally prepared monthly or weekly and do not pinpoint the specific operations that are not performing as expected. A JIT manufacturing company has short manufacturing cycles and thus requires information as problems arise on a 'real time' basis or at least on a daily basis. To overcome these problems there is a movement towards greater use of simplified non-financial measures which are directly related to manufacturing strategy and which provide fast and effective feedback. In addition greater emphasis is placed on control by direct observation (instead of relying on performance reports) by training the workers to continuously monitor quality, production flow and set-up times.

PROPOSED MODIFICATIONS

Some of the limitations of standard costing variance analysis which we have identified can be overcome by modifying the system to reflect the requirements of the new manufacturing environment. The JIT manufacturing philosophy focuses on the elimination of waste. Allowances for waste, scrap and rework should therefore be removed from standard costs and a detailed report on these items introduced. Given the constant improvement sought by JIT, standards should be regularly reviewed and tightened as improvements occur. The trends in variances should be reported, using graphical presentations, where appropriate.

'Real time' reporting

Traditionally, manufacturing performance measurements have been prepared for higher-level managers. Within an AMT environment increasing emphasis is placed on providing shop floor feedback measures for use by operating personnel in order to monitor and improve operations. For operational control purposes labour and material quantity variances should be reported in physical terms in 'real time'. Puxty and Lyall (1989), in their survey of standard costing practices, reported that some companies were using 'on-line' computers to collect information at the point of manufacture so that variances could be reported and fed into the system instantaneously. Summary variance reports can still be prepared, if required, for senior management at weekly or monthly intervals comparing actual and standard costs.

Volume-related costs

Fixed overhead volume variances should not be used for short-term operational cost control and performance measurement purposes. It is unlikely that variance analysis is appropriate for controlling those expenses which are unrelated to production volume such as equipment and facility costs. Standard cost variances may still provide useful information for controlling those costs which are volume related such as materials, energy and labour costs. We have suggested that labour costs are likely to be fixed in the short-term. Thus, in the short-term, spending will be unaffected by efficiencies/inefficiencies in the consumption of labour resources. However, in the longer term, any savings or excessive consumption in labour resources will be reflected in an increase or decrease in spending. Consequently variance analysis may provide useful information where resource spending is closely related to resource consumption. However, variances should be related to the factor which causes resource consumption rather than assuming that all variable overheads are a function of direct labour hours of input.

Misuse of variance analysis

By themselves, variance analyses and other performance measurements do not lead to excessive inventories or cause quality to deteriorate. Variances are merely tools for controlling costs. Dysfunctional consequences arise because of the way managers use these tools. If standard cost variances are modified to reflect the new manufacturing environment, and wisely used, they can still provide useful information in an advanced manufacturing environment. However, they have a less significant role to play where the majority of costs are unrelated to changes in production volume.

Introduce new performance measures

Companies operating in an advanced manufacturing environment must also introduce new performance measures which reflect their strategic manufacturing goals and which are necessary to compete successfully in today's world-wide competitive environment. The performance measures with which companies have been experimenting are non-financial and focus on such factors as quality, supplier reliability, throughput, cycle times and on-time delivery.

Activity-based cost management

Companies are beginning to experiment with new approaches for controlling fixed overhead costs which are unrelated to short-term changes in production volume. Traditional cost control systems (including variance analysis) focus primarily on controlling short-term variable resource consumption and do not provide useful information for controlling non-volume related overhead costs. In the late 1980s Cooper and Kaplan advocated a new approach for calculating more accurate product costs, called activity-based costing (ABC). It is also claimed that ABC provides a mechanism for controlling overhead costs by focusing management's attention on the underlying causes of costs (that is, the cost drivers). ABC assumes that resource consuming activities cause costs and that products incur costs through the activities they require for design, engineering, manufacturing, marketing, delivering, invoicing and servicing. By collecting and reporting on the significant activities a business engages in it is possible to understand and manage costs.

With an ABC system costs are managed in the long-term by controlling the activities which drive them. In other words the aim is to manage the activities rather than costs. By managing activities (cost drivers) costs will be managed in the long-term. Examples of cost drivers include set-up hours, number of purchase orders, number of part numbers maintained and number of suppliers.

By identifying the driving force behind non value-added activities the management accounting system is able to draw attention to those activities which, if eliminated or reduced, enable costs to be reduced in the long-term. For example, material handling costs may be driven by the number of separate parts which need to be stored and issued. Material handling costs are therefore charged to products on the basis of the number of parts required. The impact of the number of parts on cost is thus made apparent and products bear the costs proportionate to the number of parts incorporated in their design. Consequently attention is drawn to the need to standardize and reduce the number of parts. Product costs are reduced if the number of parts is reduced. Designers are thus motivated to simplify product designs and in the long run material handling costs should be reduced.

Similarly other long-run costs can be managed by focusing on activities such as set-up times and number of suppliers. The major part of cost is normally committed at the design stage. Costs should therefore be managed at this stage because by the time it comes to production and delivery it is often too late to control the costs.

SUMMARY

Standard costing systems were developed to meet the needs of a traditional manufacturing environment which is drastically different from an AMT and JIT production environment. Investment in AMTs dramatically changes the cost behaviour patterns. More of a firm's costs become fixed (and sunk) and direct labour costs represent only a small percentage of total manufacturing costs. The implications of JIT manufacturing are many, and far reaching, and standard costing variance analysis, as currently used, can encourage behaviour which is inconsistent with the objectives of JIT.

A number of writers have cast doubt on the value of standard costing in an advanced manufacturing environment and predict that standard costing will become obsolete. However, the study by Puxty and Lyall (1989) reported that standard costing continues to be used extensively in industry and is being adapted to meet the challenges presented by recent developments in production and information technologies. They also reported that only a few companies had abandoned their standard costing systems over the last ten years. Ferguson (1988) has also drawn attention to the fact that IBM's introduciton of JIT did not lead to their abandonment of standard costing.

You will recall that in Chapter 1 we noted that standard costing systems are widely used because they provide cost data for many different purposes; such as assisting in setting budgets, simplifying the task of inventory valuation, predicting future costs for use in decision-making and providing data for cost control and performance appraisal. Standard costs and variance analysis would therefore still be required for other purposes even if variance analysis was abandoned for cost control and performance appraisal purposes. In an advanced manufacturing environment variance analysis can simplify the task of inventory valuation and the preparation of profit statements and also provide feedback data for signalling the need to update standards for budgeting, cost-estimating and decision-making purposes.

It is questionable, however, whether variance analysis for cost control and performance appraisal will continue to provide useful information in a JIT and AMT environment. Variance analysis does not provide useful information for controlling those costs which are unrelated to production volume. If variance analysis continues to be used it will play a much less significant role in the control of costs and will be used for controlling only those costs which are volume-related such as direct materials, energy and labour costs. However, several studies have indicated that direct materials represent the largest percentage of total manufacturing costs. Material usage variances may therefore continue to provide useful feedback information for the control of material usage.

It is important that standard costing systems are continuously reviewed and, where appropriate, modified to reflect changes in the environment. Companies are now implementing activity-based product costing systems. Product standard costs can, however, still be computed on an activity costing basis. JIT manufacturing and AMTs are not appropriate for all companies and the limitations of standard costing which we have identified in this chapter may not apply in these companies. Standard costing has proved to be an extremely versatile tool providing, by means of a single integrated system, many different kinds of cost data for many different purposes. In some companies it may diminish in importance but standard costing systems are likely to continue to play an important role in the foreseeable future.

Questions

The chapters referred to in parentheses at the beginning of each question indicate the pre-reading which is required prior to attempting the question.

1 *[Chapters 1 and 2]* A company manufactures two products which have the following standard costs (per hundred units of output) for direct materials and direct labour:

Product 1:
98 kilos of Material M at £0.78 per kilo
10 hours in Department X at £4.20 per hour

Product 2:
33 kilos of Material N at £2.931 per kilo
9 hours in Department Y at £4.50 per hour

The predetermined production overhead rates for the two departments are:

Department X: £3.60 per direct labour hour
Department Y: £2.90 per direct labour hour

The following incomplete information is provided of actual production, costs and variances for the period:

Actual production:
Product 1: 42,100 units
Product 2: (vii)   units

176

Actual costs:
  Direct materials:
  41,200 kilos of Material M at £0.785 per kilo = £32,342
  (viii) kilos of Material N at (ix) per kilo = £23,828

  Direct labour:
  4,190 hours in Department X at £4.20 per hour = £17,598
  (x) hours in Department Y at £4.55 per hour = (xi)

  Production overhead:
  Department X   £14,763
  Department Y   (xii)

Variances:

	Material M	Material N
Direct materials		
price	(i)	£233A
usage	(ii)	£5F
total	(iii)	£228A

	Department X	Department Y
Direct labour:		
rate	(iv)	(xiii)
efficiency	(v)	£342F
total	£84F	(xiv)
Production overhead	(vi)	£142A

A denotes an adverse variance
F denotes a favourable variance

Requirements

(a) Calculate the standard costs of Products 1 and 2 (£ per hundred units, to two decimal places). (4 marks)
(b) Calculate the missing cost variances (i) to (vi) relating to Product 1 (to the nearest £). (8 marks)
(c) Calculate the missing figures (vii) to (xiv) relating to Product 2. (Calculate variances and total costs to the nearest £; production, kilos and hours to the nearest whole number; and price per kilo to two decimal places of a £). (13 marks)

(25 marks)

ACCA Level 1 Cost and Management Accounting 1
June 1990

2 *[Chapters 1 and 2]* Tardy Taxis operates a fleet of taxis in a provincial town. In planning its operations for November 1988 it estimated that it would carry fare-paying passengers for 40,000 miles at an average price of £1 per mile. However, past experience suggested that the total miles run would amount to 250% of the fare-paid miles. At the beginning of November it employed ten drivers and decided that this number would be adequate for the month ahead.

The following cost estimates were available:

Employment costs of a driver	£1,000 per month
Fuel costs	£0.08 per mile run
Variable overhead costs	£0.05 per mile run
Fixed overhead costs	£9,000 per month

In November 1988 revenue of £36,100 was generated by carrying passengers for 38,000 miles. The total actual mileage was 105,000 miles. Other costs amounted to:

Employment costs of drivers	£9,600
Fuel costs	£8,820
Variable overhead costs	£5,040
Fixed overhead costs	£9,300

The saving in the cost of drivers was due to one driver leaving during the month; she was not replaced until early December.

Requirements

(a) Prepare a budgeted and actual profit and loss account for November 1988, indicating the total profit variance. (6 marks)

(b) Using a flexible budget approach, construct a set of detailed variances to explain the total profit variance as effectively as possible. Present your analysis in a report to the owner of Tardy Taxis including suggested reasons for the variances. (14 marks)

(c) Outline any further variances you think would improve your explanation, indicating the additional information you would require to produce these. (5 marks)

(25 marks)

ICAEW P2 Management Accounting
December 1988

3 *[Chapters 1 and 2]* Chimera Ltd makes chimes, one of a variety of products. These products pass through several production processes.

The first process is moulding and the standard costs for moulding chimes are as follows:

	Standard costs per unit	£
Direct material X	7 kg @ £7.00 per kg	49.00
Direct labour	5 hours @ £5 per hour	25.00
Overhead (fixed and variable)	5 hours @ £6.60 per hour	33.00
		107.00

The overhead allocation rate is based on direct labour hours and comprises an allowance for both fixed and variable overhead costs. With the aid of regression analysis the fixed element of overhead costs has been estimated at £9,000 per week, and the variable element of overhead costs has been estimated at 60p per direct labour hour. The accounting records do not separate actual overhead costs between their fixed and variable elements.

The moulding department occupies its own premises, and all the department's overhead costs can be regarded as being the responsibility of the departmental manager.

In week 27 the department moulded 294 chimes, and actual costs incurred were:

Direct material X (2,030 kg used)	£14,125
Direct labour (1,520 hours worked)	£7,854
Overhead expenditure	£10,200

The 1,520 hours worked by direct labour included 40 hours overtime, which is paid at 50% above normal pay rates.

Requirements

(a) Prepare a report for the moulding department manager on the results of the moulding department for week 27, presenting information in a way which you consider to be most useful. (9 marks)

(b) Discuss the treatment of overheads adopted in your report and describe an alternative treatment, contrasting its use with the method adopted in your report. (6 marks)

(c) Describe the approaches used for determining standards for direct costs and assess their main strengths and weakness. (10 marks)

(25 marks)

ICAEW P2 Management Accounting
July 1986

4 *[Chapters 1–3]* A large manufacturing company with a diverse range of products is developing the use of standard costing throughout its divisions. A full standard costing system has already been implemented in Division A, including the use of mix and yield material variances, and attention has now turned to Division B where the main problem concerns labour.

Division B makes highly complex work stations which incorporate material handling, automatic controls and robotics. Manufacture is a team effort and the team specified for work station No. 26 comprises:

  2 supervisors paid £8 per hour
 10 fitters paid £6 per hour
  6 electricians paid £6 per hour
  2 electronics engineers paid £7 per hour
  4 labourers paid £4 per hour

Output is measured in standard hours and 90 standard hours are expected for every 100 clock hours. During a period the following data were recorded:

	Actual hours	Actual pay £
Supervisors	170	1,394
Fitters	820	4,920
Electricians	420	2,562
Electronics engineers	230	1,725
Labourers	280	1,120
Total	1,920	11,721

1,650 standard hours were produced

The factory director of Division B is anxious to gain the maximum information possible from the standard costing system. He sees no reason why the normal labour efficiency variance could not be divided into subvariances in order to show separately the effects of non-standard team composition and team productivity in a similar fashion to the material usage variance which can be sub-divided into mix and yield variances.

Requirements

(a) Calculate the labour rate variance. (3 marks)
(b) Calculate
         (i) The team composition variance.

    (ii)   The team productivity variance.
    (iii)   The labour efficiency variance. (11 marks)
(c)   Comment on the meaning of the variances calculated in (b) and
    their weaknesses. (6 marks)

                             (20 marks)

CIMA Stage 3 Management Accounting Techniques
November 1990

5 *[Chapters 1–3]* The budgeted income statement for one of the products
of Derwen plc for the month of May 1986 was as follows:

Budgeted income statement – May 1986

	£	£	£
Sales revenue:			
10,000 units at £5			50,000
Production costs:			
Budgeted production			
10,000 units			
Direct materials			
Material A (5,000 kg at £0.30)	1,500		
B (5,000 kg at £0.70)	3,500		
		5,000	
Direct labour			
Skilled (4,500 hours at £3.00)	13,500		
Semi-skilled			
(2,600 hours at £2.50)	6,500		
		20,000	
Overhead cost			
Fixed		10,000	
Variable (10,000 units at £0.50)		5,000	
		40,000	
Add Opening stock			
(1,000 units at £4)		4,000	
		44,000	
Deduct Closing stock		4,000	
(1,000 units at £4)			
Cost of goods sold			40,000
Budgeted profit			10,000

During May 1986 production and sales were both above budget and the following income statement was prepared:

Income statement – May 1986

	£	£	£
Sales revenue			
7,000 units at £5			35,000
4,000 units at £4.75			19,000
			54,000
Production costs			
Actual production 12,000 units			
Direct materials			
Material A (8,000 kg at £0.20)	1,600		
B (5,000 kg at £0.80)	4,000	5,600	
Direct labour			
Skilled (6,000 hours at £2.95)	17,700		
Semi-skilled			
(3,150 hours at £2.60)	8,190	25,890	
Overhead cost			
Fixed		9,010	
Variable (12,000 units at £0.625)		7,500	
		48,000	
Add Opening stock			
(1,000 units at £4)		4,000	
		52,000	
Deduct Closing stock			
(2,000 units at £4)		8,000	
Cost of goods sold			44,000
'Actual' profit			10,000

Requirements

In the above statement stock is valued at the standard cost of £4 per unit.

There is general satisfaction because the budgeted profit level has been achieved but you have been asked to prepare a standard costing statement analysing the differences between the budget and the actual performance. In your analysis, include calculations of the sales volume and sales price variances and the following cost variances; direct material price, mix, yield and usage variances; direct labour rate, mix, productivity and efficiency variances; and overhead spending and volume variances. (17 marks)

Provide a commentary on the variances and give your views on their usefulness. (5 marks)

(22 marks)

CACA Level 2 Management Accounting
December 1986

6 *[Chapters 1–4]* County Preserves produce jams, marmalade and preserves. All products are produced in a similar fashion; the fruits are low temperature cooked in a vacuum process and then blended with glucose syrup with added citric acid and pectin to help setting.

Margins are tight and the firm operates a system of standard costing for each batch of jam.

The **standard cost** data for a batch of raspberry jam are:

Fruit extract	400 kg @ £0.16 per kg
Glucose syrup	700 kg @ £0.10 per kg
Pectin	99 kg @ £0.332 per kg
Citric acid	1 kg @ £2.00 per kg
Labour	18 hrs @ £3.25 per hour
Standard processing loss 3%	

The summer of 1987 proved disastrous for the raspberry crop with a late frost and cool, cloudy conditions at the ripening period, resulting in a low national yield. As a consequence, normal prices in the trade were £0.19 per kg for fruit extract although good buying could achieve some savings. The impact of exchange rates on imports of sugar has caused the price of syrup to increase by 20%.

The *actual results* for the batch were:

Fruit extract	428 kg @ £0.18 per kg
Glucose syrup	742 kg @ £0.12 per kg
Pectin	125 kg @ £0.328 per kg
Citric acid	1 kg @ £0.95 per kg
Labour	20 hrs @ £3.00 per hour

Actual output was 1,164 kg of raspberry jam.

Requirements

(a) Calculate the ingredients planning variances that are deemed uncontrollable. (4 marks)
(b) Calculate the ingredients operating variances that are deemed controllable. (4 marks)
(c) Comment on the advantages and disadvantages of variance analysis using planning and operating variances. (4 marks)
(d) Calculate the mixture and yield variances. (5 marks)

(e)   Calculate the total variance for the batch. (3 marks)

(20 marks)

CIMA Stage 3 Management Accounting Techniques
May 1988

7   *[Chapters 1–4]* A year ago Kenp Ltd entered the market for the manufacture and sale of a revolutionary insulating material. The budgeted production and sales volumes were 1,000 units. The originally estimated sales price and standard costs for this new product were:

	£	£
Standard sales price (per unit)		100
Standard costs (per unit)		
Raw materials (Aye 10 lb at £5)	50	
Labour (6 hours at £4)	24	74
Standard contribution (per unit)		£26

Actual results were:

First year's results

	£000s	£000s
Sales (1,000 units)		158
Production costs (1,000 units)		
Raw materials (Aye 10,800 lb)	97.2	
Labour (5,800 hours)	34.8	132
Actual contribution		£26

'Throughout the year we attempted to operate as efficiently as possible, given the prevailing conditions' stated the managing director. 'Although in total the performance agreed with budget, in every detailed respect, except volume, there were large differences. These were due, mainly, to the tremendous success of the new insulating material which created increased demand both for the product itself and all the manufacturing resources used in its production. This then resulted in price rises all round'.

'Sales were made at what was felt to be the highest feasible price but, it was later discovered, our competitors sold for £165 per unit and we could have equalled this price. Labour costs rose dramatically with increased demand for the specialist skills required to produce the product and the general market rate was £6.25 per hour – although Kenp always paid below the general market rate whenever possible'.

'Raw material Aye was chosen as it appeared cheaper than the alternative material Bee which could have been used. The costs which were expected at the time the budget was prepared were (per lb): Aye, £5 and Bee, £6.

However, the market prices relating to efficient purchases of the materials during the year were:

Aye £8.50 per lb, and
Bee £7.00 per lb

Therefore it would have been more appropriate to use Bee, but as production plans were based on Aye it was Aye that was used'.

'It was not proposed to request a variance analysis for the first year's results as most of the deviations from budget were caused by the new product's great success and this could not have been fully anticipated and planned for. In any event the final contribution was equal to that originally budgeted so operations must have been fully efficient'.

Requirements

(a) Compute the traditional variances for the first year's operations. (5 marks)
(b) Prepare an analysis of variances for the first year's operations which will be useful in the circumstances of Kenp Ltd. The analysis should indicate the extent to which the variances were due to operational efficiency of planning causes. (10 marks)
(c) Using, for illustration, a comparison of the raw material variances computed in (a) and (b) above, briefly outline two major advantages and two major disadvantages of the approach applied in part (b) over the traditional approach. (5 marks)

(20 marks)

CACA P2 Management Accounting
June 1981

8 *[Chapters 1–4]* Blue Ltd manufactures a single product, the standards of which are as follows:

Standards per unit	£	£
Standard selling price		268
Less Standard cost		
Materials (16 units at £4)	64	
Labour (4 hours at £3)	12	
*Overheads (4 hours at £24)	96	172
Standard profit		96

*Total overhead costs are allocated on the basis of budgeted direct labour hours. The following information relates to last month's activities:

	Budgeted	Actual
Production and sales	600 units	500 units
Direct labour	2,400 hours at £3	2,300 hours at £3
Fixed overheads	£19,200	£20,000
Variable overheads	£38,400	£40,400
Materials	9,600 units at £4 per unit	9,600 units at £4 per unit

The actual selling price was identical to the budgeted selling price and there was no opening or closing stocks during the period.

Requirements

(a)   Calculate the variances and reconcile the budgeted and actual profit for each of the following methods:

   (i)   The traditional method.

   (ii) The opportunity cost method assuming *materials* are the limiting factor and materials are restricted to 9,600 units for the period.

   (iii) The opportunity cost method assuming *labour hours* are the limiting factor and labour hours are restricted to 2,400 hours for the period.

   (iv) The opportunity cost method assuming there are *no scarce inputs*.

(b)   Briefly explain and comment on any differences between your answers to (a) (i) to (a) (iv) above.

9   *[Chapters 1–5]* The Brio Biscuit Company has a weekly cost variance reporting system for each of its production lines. An adverse raw materials cost variance is reported when the materials content of a product exceeds the standard cost allowed. At this stage, the plant manager has to decide whether to call out an engineer to investigate whether the machine which weighs out the raw materials is still working within its design tolerances. Such an investigation will take one hour and requires that all production on the line concerned is halted. If a fault is found it will take a further two hours to reset the machine to its correct tolerances. During any stoppage the production line operatives will be idle, and the maintenance engineer will be charged at £10 per hour. If the machine is allowed to continue to operate when it should have been reset, it is estimated that the materials variance in the following week will be twice that reported in the current week.

The crunchy biscuit line is currently working at full capacity (100 hours per week) in order to satisfy the demand for this new product, and the management accounting system indicates its weekly performance is as follows:

	£
Sales (ex-factory price)	25,000
Raw materials cost	10,000
Direct labour	4,000
Indirect variable costs	1,000
Indirect fixed costs	5,000
Total cost	20,000
Profit margin	5,000

Requirements

(a) How should the manager decide whether to investigate further an adverse raw materials cost variance of

    (i) £250

    (ii) £100? (10 marks)

(b) The manager believes that a zero materials cost variance indicates that the process is certainly in control, and that a £600 variance indicates it is certainly out of control. Between those two values his belief that the process is out of control varies in direct proportion to the size of the variance. What should be his decision rule for investigating a variance, and what is the expected cost of implementing it? (10 marks).

(c) How would your above analysis be affected if resetting the machine was not certain to cure the problem, but to have only a 75% chance of so doing? (5 marks).

(25 marks)

ICAEW P2 Management Accounting
July 1989

10 *[Chapters 1–5]* From past experience a company operating a standard cost system has accumulated the following information in relation to variances in its monthly management accounts:

	Percentage of total number of variances %
1. Its variances fall into two categories:	
Category 1: those which are not worth investigating	64

Category 2: those which are worth
investigating   <u>36</u>
                           <u>100</u>

2. Of category 2, corrective action has eliminated 70% of the variances, but the remainder have continued.
3. The cost of investigation averages £350 and that of correcting variances averages £550.
4. The average size of any variance not corrected is £525 per month and the company's policy is to assess the present value of such costs at 2% per month for a period of five months.

Requirements

(a) prepare *two* decision trees, to represent the position if an investigation is:

    (i) carried out;
    (ii) not carried out;   **(12 marks)**

(b) recommend, with supporting calculations, whether or not the company should follow a policy of investigating variances as a matter of routine; **(3 marks)**
(c) explain briefly *two* types of circumstance that would give rise to variances in category 1 and *two* to those in category 2; **(6 marks)**
(d) mention any *one* variation in the information used that you feel would be beneficial to the company if you wished to improve the quality of the decision-making rule recommended in (b) above. Explain briefly why you have suggested it. **(4 marks)**

CIMA P3 Management Accounting
November 1985

11 *[Chapters 2 and 6]* A company uses material Z in several of its manufacturing processes. On 1 November, 9,000 kilos of the material were in stock. These materials cost £9,630 when purchased.

Receipts and issues of material Z during November were:

Receipts
    4 November   10,000 kilos costing £10,530
    23 November   8,000 kilos costing £8,480
Issues
    2 November   2,000 kilos to process 1
    7 November   4,500 kilos to process 2

| 20 November | 4,000 kilos to process 1 |
| 27 November | 6,000 kilos to process 3 |

The company operates a standard costing system. The standard cost of material Z during November was £1.04 per kilo.

Process 1 is exclusively concerned with the production of product X. Production information for November is as follows:

Opening work-in-process   6,000 units
 – complete as to materials; 50% complete for direct labour and overheads
Completed units   9,970
Closing work-in-process   8,000 units
 – complete as to materials; 75% complete for direct labour and overheads

The standard cost per unit of product X comprises the following:

Material Z   0.5 kilos at £1.04 per kilo
Direct labour   0.1 hours at £4.80 per hour
Overhead   absorbed on direct labour hours at £5.00 per hour

Costs (other than Material Z) incurred in process 1 during November were:

Direct labour   1,340 hours at £4.80 per hour
Overheads   £6,680

Requirements

(a) Prepare the stock account and material price variance account for Material Z for the month of November on the assumption that:

   (i) The material price variance is identified on purchase of material.
   (ii) The material price variance is identified at the time of issue of material to production (assume that the weighted average pricing method is used). (9 marks)

(b) State which of the above two methods, (a) (i) or (a) (ii), you would prefer. State briefly the reasons for your preference. (4 marks)
(c) Prepare the account for Process 1 for the month of November. (Assume that Material Z is charged to the process at standard price.) (12 marks)

(25 marks)

ACCA Level 1 Costing
December 1988

12 *[Chapters 2 and 6]* Fischer Ltd manufactures a range of chess sets, and operates a standard costing system. Information relating to the 'Spassky' design for the month of March 1985 is as follows:

1. Standard costs per 100 sets

Raw materials:	£
Plaster of Paris, 20 kg @ £8 per kg	160
Paint, ½ litre @ £30 per litre	15
Direct wages, 2½ hours @ £10 per hour	25
Fixed production overheads, 400% of direct wages	100
	300

2. Standard selling price per set, £3.80.
3. Raw materials, work in progress and finished goods stock records are maintained at standard cost.
4. Stock levels at the beginning and end of March 1985 were as follows:

	1 March 1985	31 March 1985
Plaster of Paris	2,800 kg	2,780 kg
Paint	140 litres	170 litres
Finished sets	900 sets	1,100 sets

There was no work in progress at either date.
5. Budget production and sales during the month were 30,000 sets. Actual sales, all made at standard selling price, and actual production were 28,400 and 28,600 sets respectively.
6. Raw materials purchased during the month were 5,400 kg of plaster of Paris at a cost of £43,200 and 173 litres of paint at a cost of £5,800.
7. Direct wages were 730 hours at an average rate of £11 per hour.
8. Fixed production overheads amounted to £34,120.

Requirements

Prepare for the month of March 1985:

(a) the cost ledger accounts for raw materials, work in progress and finished goods. (10 marks)
(b)   (i)   budget trading statement,
     (ii) standard cost trading statement,
     (iii) financial trading statement, and
     (iv) a reconciliation between these statements identifying all relevant variances. (14 marks)

                                                 (24 marks)

ICAEW Accounting Techniques
May 1985

Bibliography

Accounting Standards Committee. 1988. *Accounting for Stocks and Work in Progress* (SSAP 9).

Argyris, C. 1953. Human problems with budgets, *Harvard Business Review*, Jan.–Feb., 97–110. Also in Solomons, D. 1968. *Studies in Cost Analysis*. Sweet & Maxwell Ltd, London.

Atkinson, J.W. 1964. *An Introduction to Motivation*. D. Van Nostrand Co., Princeton, N.J.

Barnes, K. and Targett, P. 1984. Standard costing in distribution, *Management Accounting*, May, 26–27.

Barnes, P. 1979. Which variances are worth investigating? *Accountancy*, Dec., 80–83.

Bass, B.M. and Leavitt, H.J. 1963. Some experiments in planning and operating, *Management Science* 9: 574–585.

Bastable, C.W. and Bao, B.H. 1988. 'The fiction of sales-mix and sales quantity variances, *Accounting Horizons*, June.

Berliner, C. and Brimson, J.A. 1988. *Cost Management for Today's Advanced Manufacturing*. Harvard Business School Press.

Bierman, H., Fouraker, L.E. and Jaedicke, R.K. 1977. A use of probability and statistics in performance evaluation. In Benston, G.J. (ed.), *Contemporary Cost Accounting and Control*. Dickenson Publishing Co., U.S.A.

Bromwich, M. 1988. Costing for planning. In Cowe, R. (ed.), *Handbook of Management Accounting* (2nd edn), Gower Publishing Group Ltd, Aldershot.

Brownell, P. 1981. Participation in budgeting, locus of control and organisational effectiveness. *The Accounting Review*, October, 944–958.

Bryan, J.F. and Locke, E.A. 1967. Goal setting as a means of increasing motivation, *Journal of Applied Psychology*, June, 274–277.

Calvasina, R.V. and Calvasina, E.J. 1984. Standard costing games that managers play. *Management Accounting (USA)*, Mar., 49–51, 77.

CAMI Survey. 1988. *Management Accounting in Advanced Manufacturing Environments*. Computer Aided Manufacturing Inc., Arlington, TX, U.S.A.

Cherrington, D.J. and J.O. 1973. Appropriate reinforcement contingencies in the budget process, *Journal of Accounting Research*, Selected Studies, (supplement to vol. 2), 225–266.

Clark, J.A. 1982. A new approach to labour variances, *Management Accounting (USA)*, Dec., 36–40.

Collins, F. 1978. The interaction of budget characteristics and personality variables with budget response attitudes, *The Accounting Review*, Apr., 324–335.

Cook, D. 1968. The effect of frequency of feedback on attitudes and performance, *Journal of Accounting Research* Selected Studies (*Empirical Research in Accounting*) (supplement to vol. 6), 213–224.

Cooper, R. and Kaplan, R.S. (1988) Measure costs right: make the right decisions, *Harvard Business Review*, Sept.–Oct., 1988.

Cress, W. and Pettijohn, J. 1985. A survey of budget-related planning and control policies and procedures, *Journal of Accounting Education*, Fall, 61–78.

Demski, J.S. 1977. Analysing the effectiveness of the traditional standard costing variance model. In Benston, G.J. (ed.), *Contemporary Cost Accounting and Control*. Dickenson Publishing Co., USA.

Dopuch, N., Birnberg, J.E. and Demski, J. 1967. An extension of standard cost variance analysis, *The Accounting Review* 42(3), 526–536.

Drury, J.C. 1992. *Management and Cost Accounting* (3rd edn), Chapman and Hall Ltd, London.

Dyckman, T. 1969. The investigation of cost variances, *Journal of Accounting Research* 7(2), 215–244.

Emmons, J.P., Williams, P.F. and Arrington, C.E. 1982. A standard cost approach to receivables management, *Cost and Management (Canada)*, Nov.–Dec., 21–24.

Ferguson, P. 1988. Accounting for just in time: sorting out the conflicting advice, *Management Accounting*, Dec.

Garry, H.S. 1903. Factory costs, *The Accountant*, July, 954–961.

Gibson, B. 1990. Determining meaningful sales relational (mix) variances, *Accounting and Business Research*, 21(81): 35–40.

Greer, W.R. 1975. Standard costing in non-manufacturing activities, *Cost and Management (Canada)*, Nov.–Dec., 12–16.

Harrington, E. 1908–1909. Efficiency as a basis for operations and wages, *Engineering Magazine*, 2 parts, July and March.

Harrison, G. Charter. 1918–1919. Cost accounting to aid production, *Industrial Management*, Oct.

Harvey, D.W. and Soliman, S.Y. 1983. Standard cost variance analysis in a learning environment, *Accounting and Business Research*, Summer, 181–189.

Hasseldine, C.R. 1967. Mix and yield variances, *The Accounting Review* 42(3): 497–515.

Hofstede, G.H. 1968. *The Game of Budget Control*. Tavistock Publications Ltd., London.

Horngren, C.T. 1978. A contribution margin approach to the analysis of capacity utilization. In Anton, H.R., Firmin, P.A. and Grove, H.D. (eds). *Contemporary Issues in Cost and Managerial Accounting*. Houghton Mifflin Co., Boston, MA.

Johnson, H.T. and Kaplan, R.S. 1987. *Relevance Lost: The Rise and Fall of Management Accounting*. Harvard Business School Press.

Kaplan, R.S. 1975. The significance and investigation of cost variances: survey and extensions, *Journal of Accounting Research* 13(2): 311–337. Also in Anton, H.R., Firmin, P.A. and Grove, H.D. (eds). 1978. *Contemporary Issues in Cost and Managerial Accounting*. Houghton Mifflin Co., Boston, MA.

Kaplan, R.S. 1982. *Advanced Management Accounting* (ch. 9). Prentice-Hall, Inc., Englewood Cliffs, NJ.

Kenis, I. 1979. The effects of budgetary goal characteristics on managerial attitudes and performance, *The Accounting Review*, Oct., 707–721.

Kennedy, A. 1982. Mixes in variance analysis, *Management Accounting*, Feb., 29–31.

Koehler, R.W. 1968. The relevance of probability statistics to accounting variance control, *Management Accounting (USA)*, Oct., 35–41.

Lauderman, M. and Schaeberle, F.W. 1983. The cost accounting practices of firms using standard costs, *Cost and Management (Canada)*, July–Aug.

Longmuir, P. 1902. Recording and interpreting foundry costs, *Engineering Magazine*, Sept. 1968, 887–894.

Luh, F.S. 1968. Controlled cost: An operation concept and statistical approach for standard costing, *Accounting Review*. Jan., 123–132. Also in Rappaport, A. (ed.), 1975. *Information for Decision-Making*. Prentice-Hall, Inc., Englewood Cliffs, NJ.

Magee, R.P. 1976. Cost variance investigation models, *Accounting Review*, July, 529–545.

194   *Standard Costing*

Manes, R.P. 1983. Demand elasticities: supplements to sales budgets variance reports, *The Accounting Review*, Apr.

Martindale, A. 1982. Stirring the variances mix, *Management Accounting*, Nov., 40–42.

McClelland, D.C. 1961. *The Achieving Society*. D. Van Nostrand Co., Princeton, NJ.

Milani, K. 1975. The relationship of participation in budget setting to industrial supervisor performance and attitudes: a field study, *The Accounting Review*, Apr., 274–284.

Miles, R.E. and Vergin, R.C. 1969. Behavioural properties of variance controls. In Bruns, W.J. and De Coster, D.T. (eds), *Accounting and its Behavioural Implications*. McGraw-Hill Book Co., New York.

Mullett, M.J. 1978. Benefits from standard costing in the restaurant industry, *Management Accounting (USA)*, Aug./Sept., 47–53.

Peles, M.C. 1986. A note on yield variance and mix variance, *The Accounting Review*, Apr.

Puxty, A.G. and Lyall, D. 1989. *Cost Control into the 1990s: A Survey of Standard Costing and Budgeting Practices in the UK*. CIMA, London.

Ronen, J. 1970. Capacity and operating variances: an ex post approach, *Journal for Accounting Research* 8(1): 232–252.

Scapens, R.W. 1985. *Management Accounting: A Review of Recent Developments*. The Macmillan Press Ltd., London.

Shank, J. and Churchill, N. 1977. Variance analysis: a management orientated approach, *Accounting Review* 42(4): 950–957.

Solomons, D. 1968. The Historical Development of Costing. In Solomons, D. (ed.), *Studies in Cost Analysis* (2nd edn), Sweet & Maxwell Ltd, London.

Solomons, D. 1972. Flexible budgets and the analysis of overhead variances. In Anton, H.R. and Firmin, P.A. (eds). *Contemporary Issues in Cost Accounting*. Houghton Mifflin Co., Boston, MA.

Taylor, F.W. 1916. *The Principles of Scientific Management*. Harper and Brothers, New York.

Vroom, V.H. 1960. *Some Personality Determinants of the Effects of Participation*. Prentice-Hall, Inc., Englewood Cliffs, NJ.

Whitmore, J. 1908. Shoe factory cost accounts, *Journal of Accountancy*, May.

Wolk, H.I. and Hillman, D.A. 1972. Material mix and yield variances: a suggested improvement, *The Accounting Review*, 47(3): 549–555.

Index

195